UNLOCK YOUR HIDDEN STAR

Other Books by Vandana V. Prakash

Conquering Pain: How to Prevent It, Treat It and Lead a Better Life (co-authored with Mary Abraham)

Managing Chronic Pain (co-authored with Mary Abraham)

UNLOCK YOUR HIDDEN STAR

Guiding Children with Learning Disabilities

VANDANA V. PRAKASH

First published in India by Harper Learning 2026
An imprint of HarperCollins *Publishers*
HarperCollins *Publishers* India, Cyber City,
Building 10-A, Gurugram, Haryana – 122002, India
www.harpercollins.co.in

2 4 6 8 10 9 7 5 3 1

P-ISBN: 978-93-7307-123-7
E-ISBN: 978-93-7307-061-2

Typeset in 12/15.2 Adobe Garamond Pro
by HarperCollins *Publishers* India Pvt. Ltd

Printed and bound at
Saurabh Printers Pvt. Ltd.

This book is produced from independently certified FSC® paper to ensure responsible forest management.

HarperCollins *Publishers*, Macken House, 39/40 Mayor Street Upper,
Dublin 1, D01 C9W8, Ireland

To my parents,
Shakuntala & Prahlad

Contents

Section III: Evaluation and Management of Learning Disabilities

Foreword

WнEN A CHILD is born, it is usually a time of joy for the entire family, with a lot of expectations and celebrations. How a new parent responds to the little one depends on a lot of factors. If, to this, is added the news of a disability in the baby, the joy turns into mourning: families usually respond to it as if it were the death of their dreams.

Learning disability (LD) is an overarching term for various types of learning problems observed in children and adolescents. It is a behavioural and developmental condition, and occurs due to intellectual disability, neurological dysfunction or environmental deprivation. Learning disability affects the ability of the brain to send, receive and process information. A person with LD may have difficulties in reading, writing, speaking, listening, understanding mathematical concepts and overall comprehension.

Learning disability includes a group of disorders, such as dyslexia, dyspraxia, dyscalculia and dysgraphia—each type may co-exist with each other at the same time. A child with LD not only has to deal with debilitating academic repercussions caused due to the condition, but also with a lot of social and psychological problems, impacting overall functioning.

A simple analogy for the same would be to imagine driving a car and seeing that the road ahead has really tough traffic. What you envisage in such a turn of events is getting stuck in this traffic again and again, and blaming yourself for what has happened to you. For a child diagnosed with LD, his/her processing abilities see the incoming information (having to read, write, calculate, etc.) as chaotic, difficult-to-negotiate traffic.

If the child gets through it in a slow and frustrating manner, instead of blaming the child, the wiser idea would be to find another way out; another way to teach.

The LD movement in India is quite a recent one when compared to the high-income countries where LD movements started much earlier. The existence of difficulties caused by LD was brought out openly in the Hindi movie *Taare Zameen Par* (2007). This movie was an eyeopener and played a major role in providing awareness to Indian parents and schools. The important message this movie conveys is: it is not that the child tends to avoid studies and is casual or carefree, but that there can be high chances of one or more clinical conditions which the child may be suffering from, and therefore is not able to express his/her problem adequately.

There is thus a need for early identification and appropriate management. Recent Indian studies point out that about 5–15 per cent of children are diagnosed with LD—with more cases reported in boys than in girls. The cases presently outnumber the available experts or professionals who provide care for children with LD in India.

I sincerely congratulate Dr Vandana V. Prakash for a laudable effort and see this book as an opportunity to disseminate the different aspects related to learning and learning disability. This book has been meticulously curated, covering different aspects of LD, helping children and parents to understand the varied layers of problems faced by a child diagnosed with LD. It describes, in a simple and lucid way, the different aspects—such as neurological, psychosocial, or psychological—that hinder the overall process of development and growth. The use of anecdotes and real-life examples have made it all the more interesting, making it accessible to the general population in the most attractive manner.

The contents of the chapters are sensitive to the needs of students. I commend the author of this book for the insights, and for including assessments and remediation, with special consideration for teachers and parents. I recommend her efforts to a diverse readership as an intellectual resource and inspiration.

Dr Rajesh Sagar
MD, MNAMS, FIMSA, FRCP (Edin.)
Professor
Department of Psychiatry
All India Institute of Medical Sciences New Delhi

Preface

DISABILITIES, WHETHER PHYSICAL, mental or intellectual, have been described from time immemorial in both spoken and written literature—as seen in folklore, epics, drama, fairy tales, novels, novellas and nearly every form of narrative. Most of us have read the famous story of a disabled man, Quasimodo, in Victor Hugo's *The Hunchback of Notre Dame* (first published in 1831). Our very own Indian epic Ramayana has a hunchbacked character Manthra. And in the Mahabharata, we find the blind king Dhritarashtra. Unfortunately, any kind of differently abled character in all of the above, was usually attributed nefarious intent linked in some inexplicable way to misdemeanour. Most of these characters were not shown any compassion or kindness in the narrative. Since these stories have always been part of a growing child's reading or storytelling, it has not augured well in forming a sympathetic attitude towards the differently abled. Over centuries, the differently abled have been shunned, marginalized or simply ignored in the civilized world.

Regrettably, despite advancement in science, the moralistic tone still persists.

The word 'disability' has had a long and complicated history. Initially it was understood in a religious and didactic connotation, likening it to one's 'karmas' or moral deeds, past corrupt actions of parents and even witchcraft. Later views held disability as tragedy or charity, where the disabled was considered a figure of pity. The Social Adapted Model considered disability as limitations in a world of the able-bodied, while the economic model linked it to loss of productivity and its effect on the individual, employer and society in general. The expert/professional model was akin to the medical model, with the view of seeing disability as an impairment and providing help to improve the health condition of the disabled.

The medical model viewed it as fixing of physical and mental attributes, whereas the social model saw it as an imposition of limitations in a society of the ablest. The individual's performance was gauged by their ability to perform the physical tasks of daily life and their ease in doing so. This was termed as physiological functional capacity or PFC. With advancing years there is a natural decline in PFC, be it cognitive or physical, leading to frailty in a person, and thereby labelled as disabled. Thus, it can be said that the difficulty in physical, sensory, developmental, mental, cognitive or intellectual capacity—or a combination of several of these issues—makes it complicated, and most of the times leads to poor adjustment of the disabled in the social milieu. The empowering model and later the consumer model considered disability as 'rights-based', where the individual and the family were allowed to decide the course of treatment—thereby relegating the professional to the position of service provider instead of decision maker.

All these debates or conjectures finally were laid aside with the announcement of the 'Declaration on the Rights of Disabled Persons' on 9 December 1975, by the General Assembly of the United Nations. Since then, the disabled, including those suffering from learning disability or LD, have been given legal rights.

The term 'learning disability'—initially coined as 'word blindness' by a German neurologist Adolf Kussamaul—was first used almost a century and a half ago in 1877. A decade later, the term 'dyslexia' was phrased by another German, Rudolf Berlin. He described dyslexia as 'very great difficulty in interpreting written or printed symbols'. Gradually, many medical professionals—including ophthalmologists, physicians, psychiatrists and those from other branches of medicine—began describing their own experiences of dealing with individuals who had word blindness or dyslexia, despite having high intelligence, no visual deficits or hearing impairments.

Although the first childhood reading difficulties report was published in 1905 in the United States (USA), it took more than five decades before Samuel A. Kirk used the term 'learning disability' in 1963. Another six years passed for USA's law on Children with Specific Learning Disabilities Act to be passed. It was later included in their Education of the Handicapped Act of 1970. Another two decades passed before the word 'handicap' was replaced by 'disability'.

This book on learning disability is not just another treatise on information giving. It has been written for two major purposes. Children with LD struggle with academics despite having an intelligent and incisive mind. They have many abilities, attributes and aptitudes that tend to get buried under the weight of academic curriculum. Empathic dealing brings out the best from the child. As has laughingly been said by Mark Twain, 'All schools, all colleges, have two great functions: to confer and to conceal valuable knowledge.' We all know that knowledge has never been, nor ever will lie, embedded only in books. Books are but a reflection of observations and recognition of phenomena that have been recorded for posterity. Wisdom lies in using an amalgamation of books and practical training, making learning a rich and valuable experience and, thereby enabling a learning-disabled child to grow up like other children—with dignity, self-respect and pride in self.

A second and equally important reason was that a fair number of children came to me with emotional disturbances, and later it was discovered that the primary problem was LD. Early identification and prompt assistance given to them could have facilitated their academics and prevented, or at least reduced, any subsequent distress. Psychological rebuilding takes a long time and sadly, at times, leaves significant scars on the psyche that may never heal. Remediation work, also, cannot be effective in the absence of emotional well-being.

Thus, this book is meant for parents, teachers, professionals and non-medical persons to enable them to recognize the signs and symptoms of LD. It would help in seeking professional aid at the earliest. The book is therefore written in an easy and friendly style, interspersed with actual cases seen by me in the three decades of my professional life. The identity of the child and parents have been kept anonymous and the names used are fictitious.

The book has been arranged in a systematic manner, with three major sections. It begins with an actual case, followed by the expected developmental growth of children from age 7 to the adolescence stage ranging from 11 to 17 years. The second section of the book defines the learning process, LD, types of LDs and the associated psychological problems that are frequently seen in children. The third and final section of the book has five chapters. The first chapter is devoted to the psychological tests needed to assess learning disabilities. It is followed by effective remediation techniques that can be used for reducing disabilities, and efficacious psychotherapeutic methods for associated psychological problems that accompany LD. A chapter each is addressed to parents and teachers for managing the child at home and in school, respectively. The very last chapter is an overview of the legal status of disability in India.

We are aware that each one of us has limited resources and cannot personally reach a large number of affected children and their parents. Neither can innumerable forays be made into society to change its attitudes, prejudices, stereotypes, biases and mindsets. Instead of casting verbal stones, let us understand the suffering that children with LD go through personally, and their parents with them. We can make an attempt to understand and view them with compassion, sympathy and empathy, and through this book travel together towards a humane journey of acceptance and nurturance of the learning disabled.

Dr Vandana V. Prakash

SECTION I

Marking Child Development

Sweety

Excerpts from the diary of a mother with a learning-disabled child

'MUMMY YOU DON'T love me,' said my 6-year-old daughter Sweety. 'Of course, I do,' was my instant indignant response. Apart from being startled by her words, it bewildered me that a child who till yesterday was cuddling and kissing me all the time when I was at home, should come up with this remarkable statement. On being cajoled she elaborated that I did not love her because I was sending her to school. This was another bombshell, dropped so nonchalantly. School till yesterday was fun and play, then what had happened so suddenly? I sat her on my knees, hugged her and softly persuaded her to reveal what lay behind these words and her unhappiness.

She said that the school was 'bad' and 'I'm not happy' and 'my teacher does not love me anymore'. So I further coaxed her to tell me more as to what was making her so miserable. She reasoned with me that since she had already learnt the alphabet, why did she need to go to school? The teachers did not know anything and could not even *recite the alphabet in order. I smiled at this. The school was familiar to me because my elder daughter, Tina, was already a student there and was a year ahead in class to the younger one. I knew their pattern of teaching. The school used the Playway and Montessori methods of teaching.*

In fact, when Tina had joined the school, she was already familiar with alphabets and numbers by rote from her kindergarten classes. The teacher at the current school had requested me not to teach her at home as they followed the Playway and Montessori methods of teaching alphabets and phonetics. However, Tina would come home and recite and read from the alphabet books. Sweety would hear her recite, and had learnt by rote whatever Tina had learnt in school, right from the kindergarten days. In fact, I would often joke that half my time was saved by both the girls learning simultaneously.

Well, I presumed wrongly, as the time to come told me a different story. I had presumed, again wrongly, that perhaps Sweety was bored…as she was ahead of others in the class. So I stopped teaching her at home completely. I felt that the newness of learning should be maintained, else the child would develop negativity towards the school and studies. After a week of suspended teaching at home there was another outburst from my daughter. Now she just refused to go to school and cried copiously. She kept repeating that no one loved her. This rejection of the school and subsequent refusal to attend school was definitely worrisome. I was perturbed too, as I was sorely missing my laughing and joyful child. I decided to visit the school and speak to the class teacher to enquire about the reasons behind my child refusing to go to school.

The mother had repeatedly consulted me professionally about how to help her child. School refusal was not only worrisome for her, but as a working mother it put considerable pressure on her as she felt guilty about neglecting her child. Her husband had repeatedly asked her to leave her job and concentrate on bringing up the children. Soon after, she did leave her job. As I was closely associated with her and her daughter, I had requested her to maintain a diary and write in first person about how she was coping with the difficulties presented to her by her daughter.

Well, when I went to meet the teacher, she was teaching the class phonetics which Sweety had learnt quite well orally. However, as the teacher was now teaching them to write, I saw a discrepancy between the oral recitation and writing ability. Orally what Sweety knew so well, she was unable to put down on paper, as per the instructions of the teacher. The class teacher was an elderly lady with years of experience in handling children. I confided in her about my daughter's reaction and her refusal to go to school. The teacher too was disturbed and comforted me by urging me not to worry. She further asked me to check Sweety's copies every day and to reinforce at home whatever was being taught in school. It was a fair request, and I was relieved that perhaps my daughter was just taking time to learn what came easily to other children. It was only a case of developmental delay as suggested by Dr P.

Being a diligent and conscientious mother, I laboured to teach her phonetics again. We started practising phonetics every day. Together we plodded on, not only with phonetics but also writing alphabets and numbers. It was apparent that she had picked up phonetics but was getting confused between certain similar sounding phonemes.[1] For instance, she would confuse between sounds (both in English and Hindi) such as 'ma' and 'na', 'da' and 'dha', 'pa' and 'pha' and so on. Later I saw that she had difficulty in incorporating the sounds into words. A repeated mistake was writing 'no' as 'on', 'fat' as 'pat'. There was confusion between the basic sounds of each vowel—as seen in 'bat', 'bit', 'bot', 'bet' and 'but'. There was more confusion in the spelling of words where two vowels ran together, like 'ae', 'ous', 'ei', 'ie'.

However, with consistent repetition, she did manage to learn many of the sounds and incorporate them correctly in usage as well. Nonetheless, if I left a gap in her practising the phonetics and writing them, there would be more mistakes in both the classwork and homework. I realized that whatever happened in my personal life on a day-to-day basis, I needed to give her unswerving reinforcement of learnt material.

This led to implementation of one of the ground rules at home, of having dedicated study hours. Both the children were to study for an hour every day. To avoid any distractions, I would unhook the phone and switch-off the television. Even if one had finished with her studies and the other was yet to complete the homework, she was encouraged to keep herself busy by doing artwork like painting, sketching and colouring. All three of us would leave the study room together. My daughter started performing better in class and no longer made a fuss about going to school.

Her diary was like a bouquet, and I have extracted several flowers that I found interesting and which showed her creativity as a mother.

On one occasion, when Sweety was in Class IV, she had to write a mathematics test. It was on the concept of time and fractions. The clock and fractions were being taught together, primarily as halves and quarters. She was able to answer questions in a certain pattern, but when the same question was asked in the reverse she would be lost. For example, 9.15 was read correctly but if asked 'what is quarter past nine?' or 'quarter to nine', she would be completely at sea. This confusion prompted me to start using visual aids. So, the concept of time was taught with the help of an actual watch, fractions by cake pieces, biscuits and other edible goods. While learning the concept, the food items became reinforcers to motivate her to study.

Some of these personal experiences made me wise about dealing with her disability. I met several other parents who too were witnessing similar occurrences. A mother I met, underwent training as a special educator to help her child. Now with her child in college she was using her skills to help underprivileged children who could not afford the fee of a special educator. On one occasion, while we were comparing notes, she asked me to maintain a diary of my experiences to share with parents facing similar tribulations. I told her that I was writing a diary at the behest of a professional, as I had found her suggestion sensible, useful and doable.

A final and last peep into her diary that inspired me to write about learning disability (LD), before I close it forever, for this book.

When I look back, I can summarize this journey as being fraught with struggles, tears and joys too. Today as I helped my daughter don her black coat for her first case assistance in the Supreme Court of India, I realized that if handled well not only can children with LD be helped, but also the family can navigate the problems without getting dysfunctional and distressed.

This book seeks to, as simply as possible, explain the concept of 'learning disability' and how to deal with it for the assistance of parents, teachers, special educators, educationists, psychologists, professionals and the general public. So let us begin our journey together. Before we talk about LD, let me describe the developmental growth between the ages of 7+ to adolescence (7 to 16 years). This is the age range which we will be focusing upon in this book.

1
Developmental Growth

CHILDREN CAN BE effectively helped if they are understood. The best people to understand them are of course the parents. But the teachers who spend a year and sometimes more than a year with the student, could also have a rough idea about the developmental growth of the child. There are definite markers of growth, and each stage has certain characteristics. Here the developmental markers in cognitive, emotional and social, and moral development are described. However, before we come to these areas, it is important, particularly for the parents, to understand the temperamental traits of their child.

Temperament refers to the characteristics and personality traits we are born with, indicating that they are innate and enduring. For instance, children, who are nervous, shy and respond badly to loud noise, show innate tendencies to anxiety. When these children grow up, they may exhibit higher anxiety than others and may even be susceptible to anxiety disorders.

Thomas et al. distinguished nine temperamental traits and three temperamental types.[1] Let me describe the temperamental traits first.

Activity Level

This shows the amount of movement and body activity of an infant. From early months the active child would be seen kicking its legs and showing more general movements. Later, the child would be rolling all over the bed; when older, the child would race around the house and generally would be found to fidget, squirm or be unable to sit quietly. The child would be found shifting from one activity to another, perhaps not finishing the task at hand. Less active children can be made to sit quietly and kept engaged in activities like playing with toys that require precision or reading a book.

Biological Regularity

This refers to the regularity of the biological functions of the child and includes the sleep–wake cycle, hunger and bowel elimination. Children with regular biological rhythm have consistent timings of eating and sleeping, and follow a more or less fixed schedule. Conversely, children who show lack of regularity, have varied timings and refuse to settle into a schedule. This may be upsetting for the parents too, as they are unable to regulate their own biological rhythms to match the child's.

Adaptability

This refers to the rapidity of adaptation to changed environment, i.e., the ability to overcome an initial refusal response. Children with slow adaptability show poor responses to changes. They may not like surprises, are unable to cope with variations in schedule, find travelling and new places threatening, and fret easily. Such children prefer a fairly fixed schedule and show discomfort if the schedule gets altered. Children with good adaptability rather enjoy changes, feel excited and like the challenges offered by new circumstances.

Approach/Withdrawal

This is the reaction of the infant to a new or strange person, or an unfamiliar situation. Children with a high approach response take well to the novelty of the situation. They become easily friendly with strangers, get excited by new toys and are willing to participate. Reticent children withdraw from strangers, may hide behind their parents, are not willing to try out new experiences and may take time to familiarize with a new toy when reassured that it is harmless.

Sensitivity Threshold

This is when sensitivity of the child is gauged by its reaction to offensive stimuli such as sound, temperature, taste, texture and crowds. Sensitive children are fussy about food, unable to wear rough or certain kind of clothes and are sensitive to others' moods. Such children cry in sympathy with another crying child, or feel anxious when someone else is scolded. On the other hand, the less sensitive type can adjust with any kind of food, clothing and sleeping arrangements and is not easily affected by others' emotions.

Intensity of Emotional Response

This is gauged by the intensity of the reaction of the child to any situation. A child with an intense response will cry loudly and lustily, and express pleasure and displeasure strongly. The child with less intensity is more likely to whimper and be reserved in expression of emotions, be they positive or negative. Most parents, and later teachers, may have to decipher their emotions by understanding the subtle changes seen on their faces and their body language.

Quality of Mood

This is estimated by the kind of mood most often exhibited. The child could be cheerful and laughing (positive mood), or crying and fussing (negative mood). Children with an upbeat mood are naturally optimistic and do not get easily upset by trivial happenings. On the other hand, the naysayers are unable to find the silver lining and tend to negate even positive happenings.

Distractibility

This is judged by the ease with which a child can be distracted in unexpected situations. Those children who are easily distractible, may also be observers. For example, a small item dropped in the room that has escaped everyone's notice, may be spotted by them. However, the less distractible child has a narrow focus that makes their attention span better, and they actually concentrate and complete a given task.

Persistence/Attention Span

This is the tenacity and persistence seen in a child to keep up with a difficult task. Children with high persistence seem doggedly attached to an activity and even an idea. It is difficult to dislodge them even when they know that the activity no longer is fruitful or wise. Conversely, the less persistent ones can easily be distracted by another activity or idea.

~

These temperamental traits continue, with some modifications, into adulthood. Personal experiences and environment play a strong role in shaping how we adapt. Nonetheless, temperamental traits continue to rule us as well. The permutations and combinations of these temperamental traits determine the temperamental type. Three temperament types—easy, difficult and slow to warm up—were identified by Thomas and Chess.[2]

The Easy or Flexible Type

As the words themselves suggest, children with such a temperament are easy to handle. These children have a regular biological rhythm, are adaptable to change, can adjust in most circumstances, normally remain cheerful and even their expressed distress is not of high intensity. However, such children may experience and indicate deep feelings through minimal show of emotions. Also, they may react poorly and upset other children.

Difficult or Feisty Children

These children are a direct contradiction to easy children. Difficult or feisty children create a lot of stress for their parents and caregivers. They do not follow any single pattern of behaviour. They also do not have a regular biological rhythm so their sleeping, eating, bowel movements are varied, making it difficult for parents to train them. They are fussy in nearly everything, so what may appear to be a favourite today may not be so tomorrow. Normally, they have more 'bad' moods, and cry and howl loudly. They are not easy to soothe and, from an early age, show temper tantrums. Most parents feel exasperated with them but showing anger or resentment upsets the child further. If handled with patience and understanding, they learn to adjust.

Slow to Warm-Up or Fearful Children

Such children are the shy and timid kind, and are normally always on the fringe. Like difficult children, these children too may or may not show consistency in their biological rhythms. But unlike difficult children, they are slow to adapt to new situations, take time to adjust, are wary of strangers, cling to caregivers and can be seen hiding behind them, peeping out to understand the threat involved before venturing out. They take time to become friends with the peer group, and even then, they avoid being the centre of attention. Once they feel comfortable, they adapt well.

Developmental Growth from 7+ Years On: Understanding the Cognitive/Intellectual Growth of the Child

Piaget divided cognitive development into four stage, namely: Sensorimotor (Birth to 18–24 months); Preoperational (2+ years to 7 years); Concrete operational (7 to 11 years); and Formal operations (11+ years to adulthood).[3] Here, only the last two operations will be described, as LD is diagnosed at 7+ years.

Concrete operational: During this stage, children are generally in Class I or II to V or VI. This stage is characterized by replacement of egocentric thinking by 'operational' thoughts. Egocentric thinking is when children see themselves as the centre of the universe and cannot understand another's point of view. Operational thoughts are the ability to attend to information coming from the environment and to understand another's point of view. They can cognitively serialize, order and group objects based on the similarity between them.

Two major developments, *conservation* and *reversibility*, are seen in this period. *Conservation* refers to the logical ability to recognize that a certain quantity will remain the same, despite change in shape, size or container. To illustrate, if two similar-sized glasses carry an equal amount of liquid and the contents of one glass are transferred into a shorter, more rounded glass then the child who has attained conservation would say that the amount remains the same. However, the child who has not attained conservation will say that the first glass has more liquid.

Reversibility refers to the ability to recognize that numbers and objects change and can also be returned to their original state. For instance, water can be changed to ice and, in reverse, ice can change back to water.

So, primarily the cognitive development seen during this stage is development of:

a) Logical thinking (still rudimentary);
b) Recognition of conversion of numbers, mass and weight; and
c) Classification of objects by recognizing the similarities and putting them in order.

At this juncture, appropriate logical thinking has developed and that can be applied to new situations and conclusions. This is called *inductive thinking*. The conclusions drawn can then be used to generalize to other situations. Thus, the child can arrange and rearrange mental images and symbols, understand simple differences and similarities of objects and can do reverse counting. For example, the child knows that cat and mouse are both animals, or that mango and banana are both fruits. The child can also answer questions such as which day comes before Tuesday or before Friday, and can do reverse counting from 20 to 1.

Formal operations: This is the final stage of cognitive development and starts from the early adolescence (11+ years to adulthood) period. The child's logical and rational thinking is now on a firmer footing. The child can think in abstract terms of a higher order. For example, if asked to name the similarities between concepts like iron and silver, they can readily answer that both are metals. By this time *deductive reasoning* and the ability to define *abstract concepts* have also developed.

Deductive reasoning is the process of reasoning from one or more statements to reach a logical conclusion. To illustrate, the following statements in sequence—'all men can walk', 'John can walk', so 'John is a man'—arrive at a logical conclusion. On the other hand, *abstract concepts* are ideas that have no physical form. Common examples for abstract thinking include the ability to define concepts like love, justice, liberty, success and democracy.

Understanding Emotional and Social Growth

Emotions are visible right from the birth of the child. Usually, the first emotion noticeable is distress or crying. Any form of discomfort—from hunger, wetness, sleepiness or any unpleasantness—is signalled by crying. As the child grows older, other emotions like responding to a smile, expressing anger and frustration, and even laughter and surprise, become evident. With maturity, the response to a smile becomes a social smile.

Say, by 4 to 6 years of age, other emotions such as envy, guilt, insecurity, humility and confidence, are visible. The growing child's appraisal and perception of experiences, form the building blocks of social communications and social relationships, which in turn depend upon *emotional regulation* and *emotional expressions*.

Emotional regulation or self-regulation is the ability to check and change which emotions one has, when to respond to them, and also how one experiences and expresses them. Emotional expressions include self-expressions as well as reading the expressions of others—both abilities directly relate to the ability to engage in social relationships.

Now let us see how mood is regulated by one's temperament. A person with a cheerful disposition would not react too adversely to minor irritants, whereas an opposite reaction would be seen in a person with a sad disposition. A person who is habitually irritable would express anger at the slightest pretext. However, temperamental traits to some extent do get modified by the experiences that a child gains in the family and the immediate environment. So, a child brought up in a warm, secure environment will have better mood regulation and would express emotions similarly.

A child who has lacked warmth, and is brought up in a restrictive home environment where expectations far exceed the capacity, is bound to grow up with a sense of failure and frustrations. Their emotional reactions would be overwhelmingly negative. In case the familiar environment does not provide substitute or alternative emotional support and warmth, say from a sibling, cousins, aunts, uncles, grandparents, or perhaps a neighbour, the child's socialization process may remain impoverished, and the child may actually have poor emotional balance.

Once school life begins, the child quickly learns that an emotional outburst in front of others is socially unacceptable behaviour. Take the example of expressing anger or frustration in front of the teacher. Obviously, it is unacceptable behaviour, as compared to expressing feelings in the presence of the peer group. Emotions are expressed most freely at home and with parents. Hence the oft-heard lament of parents that the child is well-behaved everywhere except at home. Also, at this age children learn to verbalize their emotions much more than acting them out physically. One can expect the child to say rather than enact 'I'm happy because I got a new friend', instead of jumping up and down, or 'don't make me angry' rather than kicking or hitting.

Since by now better self-regulation and emotional expression has been learnt, the child is able to behave in socially appropriate ways. This increases social interactions that help children to adjust in society.

The adolescence stage sees further emotional transformations, both due to growing intellectual and physical changes as well as sharper understanding of environmental cues. Intellectual growth alters the perspective of many observations and interests, and amends one's view of self and of the world. The physical changes normally seen are gain in height, changes in the shape of the body and the growth of secondary sexual characteristics. If there is a match between the image the person carries of oneself and the actual bodily changes, then the teenager feels emotionally more comfortable.

Environmental changes that an adolescent can face are adjustments in the family dynamics, school experiences, peer group, interaction with teachers, neighbours and so on. Agreeable dealings may modify unfriendly emotions to pleasant ones as social reactions are powerful transforming agents. Over a period of time, these responses get conditioned and generalized to many situations and people. Those who are able to meet and match the expectations of others continue to have pleasant emotions, while the reverse holds for those who are unable to do so.

Self-concept: Our thoughts and feelings about how we perceive ourselves physically, socially, emotionally and personally, make up our self-concept. It is our answer to 'who am I?' So, it is the sum total of our own observations and knowledge about how we behave, what attributes of personality we have, what are our capabilities, as well as our attitudes and reactions towards life, people and the environment in which we live. Our self-concept starts developing from early childhood (2–6 years) and rapidly grows in the middle years (7–12 years) of childhood and adolescence (13–18 years).

Carl Rogers said that self-concept was not a static state but was active, dynamic and malleable.[4] He added that three components constitute self-concept namely self-image, self-esteem and ideal self.

Self-image: It refers to the way we view ourselves. When asked to describe ourselves, we might do so by physically portraying ourselves as being tall or having brown hair and black eyes, etc. Socially, we might normally talk of the various roles we play as a son, a daughter, an employee or a spouse. Personally, we might identify our personality traits as introverted, helpful, compassionate, angry and so on. It is not necessary that how we perceive ourselves coincides with how others perceive us.

Self-esteem: According to Carl Rogers this refers to how we value ourselves. Our self-esteem also depends upon how others see us. When we compare ourselves to others and vice versa, and find ourselves better at something than others, our self-esteem is high. However, the reverse stands equally true. When the comparisons are unfavourable to us, the self-esteem is likely to be low.

Ideal self: The ideal self, according to Rogers, is the self we would like to become. When it coincides with, or is at least similar to, our real self, our self-esteem is high. Conversely, if the disparity between ideal self and real self is too wide, then self-esteem is low.

Identity formation stage in adolescence: The self is an important factor during adolescence, as at this stage identity formation takes place. Identity is a personal sense of self that makes us feel ourselves as being integrated and cohesive, and it remains with us throughout our lives. This self is shaped by our personal experiences and interaction with others, all of which help form our values, beliefs, behaviours and morals. Again, as in childhood, positive strokes in life are encouraging and strengthen our sense of self, of being in control and independent. On the other hand, when self is poorly integrated, the adolescent grows up being unsure, apprehensive and under-confident. This leaves them confused about their identity, leading to **role confusion** or **identity diffusion**. They would be more susceptible to delinquent behaviour, gender-related identity disorder and borderline psychotic episodes.[5]

Identity formation stage is characterized by many changes in the adolescent's psyche and behaviour, but here only two major changes would be described. Erikson attributed a stable identity with the emergence of fidelity. Fidelity is the ability to maintain freely given loyalties, despite there being contradictions to one's own value system. Hence at this age, adolescents are seen to belong to certain groups, as seen in 1960s and 1970s when the popularity of the hippie culture was at its peak. This brings us to the second major transformation in adolescents, the importance of the peer group.

Peer group: The nature of friendship is modified during adolescence. The 'buddy' relationships in childhood are usually between the same gender and depend more upon the time spent together and the helping nature of the person. But in adolescence, friendships depend more upon commonly shared interests or values. Hence the groups or cliques formed are insular and even homogeneous. The group members usually are emotionally supportive towards each other with shared secrets, loyalties, closeness and intimacy. The allegiance between members grows multifold when opposite gender attractions begin, as the need to confide, seek advice, handle stresses and resolve conflicts is managed with the help of the group. The closeness that was once shared with parents, is now taken over by the peer group.

Not everything is satisfactory in adolescent friendships. Peer groups—whether intentionally or unintentionally—exert pressure on their members. When peer pressure drives the adolescent to be goal-directed, motivated, helpful and empathic, then the adolescent grows into a responsible adult. However, when peer pressure is exerted—especially on susceptible adolescents who carry fear of rejection by the group—the persuasion to experiment with risk-taking behaviours can easily be accomplished. Even if uncomfortable, to please the group, susceptible adolescents may do rash driving, use and abuse substances like alcohol, drugs and cigarettes. Not all adolescents grow irresponsible due to these experiments, but the poorly integrated ones may become addicted, or worse, develop psychopathological disorders.

Case Notes from My Diary: Nikita

A 19-year-old tall and well-groomed young woman named Nikita came to the hospital to meet me. She appeared anxious as well as embarrassed. On being asked in what way she needed help, she at once said that she was not sure. As I waited for her to speak, she clarified further that she was not sure whether she needed any help or was just wasting my time. I invited her to sit and encouraged her to tell me what prompted her to seek help.

She reiterated about her lack of certainty, so I just waited and gave her more time to adjust to the idea of consulting a clinical psychologist. She then began about her school life where she had performed below average in academics. In junior classes she was teased for being the tallest person in class and had been variously nicknamed as 'Eiffel

Tower' and 'Qutub Minar'. But as she grew older the teasing became related to her studies. She heard jibes like 'your brain has slid to your knees' or 'information takes longer time to reach the brain'. Though she had friends, she felt that they had not vociferously protected her.

As she was not academically sound, she thought of an alternative career. Upon discussion with her mother, who emphasized that her height was her asset, she thought of modelling as a career. Since she found ready support in her mother, she felt ambitious enough to try for beauty pageants. Throughout those years, her continuous thought was that she would prove her worthiness to her classmates by making a name for herself. Her fame would eclipse all the academically brilliant fellow students.

She started training to walk the ramp. In one such beauty pageant organized by a club she won the first prize. Despite her achievement, the inferiority feelings did not die. To boost her morale, she started thinking of others as being less than her. She would fantasize about the class, particularly boys, being in awe of her. This brought some comfort to her and momentarily she would feel superior to others. Slowly her friendships dwindled away as the reality of poor academics and her daydreams were too much at variance with each other.

Now she was in college. However, she realized that the only time she did not feel inferior to others was when she was putting them down in her mind. She became concerned about her thinking process after winning another beauty pageant. This time her thoughts were about her special friend. She felt 'he was good for nothing', 'not as smart as her', 'once she was famous, she would ditch him' and other such thoughts. However, when this special friend happened to meet another girl from the same class and they had coffee together, she felt so jealous that she cried for hours together. She did try to reason out why she had felt bad, as after all he was not of her standard. Anyways, she had planned to break up with him once college got over, despite knowing that he did care for her. That is when she realized *that perhaps this type of thinking had not helped her at all. She had continued to feel less than the others.*

On psychological tests she showed poor self-concept, low self-esteem, relationship issues and poor self-image. This case shows the importance of growing-up years being vital for a child to build a positive image of self, being able to make and maintain social relationships and learning to value people in life.

Moral development: Starting from the middle years of childhood, moral development starts and grows strong by late adolescence and adulthood. Morality is defined as conformity to shared standards, rights and duties. Lawrence Kohlberg described three levels of moral development.[6] The first level is the pre-conventional morality seen in young children (3–7 years) who comply with the obedience required and punishment doled out by their parents. Rightness and wrongness depends upon the reward and punishment received for their behaviour. The second level is role conformity. Here, children (8–13 years) learn to conform to the roles they are expected to play to gain approval, and learn to maintain social relationships. In the third level, which is considered the highest one, the child, or rather the adolescent (14 years to adulthood), learns to adhere to self-accepted moral principles.

The adolescent by now has well-developed ethical standards that may or may not comply with societal norms. When conflict arises between two incompatible, socially accepted standards, the person learns to choose what the conscience dictates. Though most people adhere to the accepted social norms, the adolescence stage is marked by questioning these said norms. Thus, as the adolescent grows older, the norms and ethics which do not harm others are accepted. These may or may not be in consonance with prevalent morality of the society.

Dear readers, by now you are well-versed with the various expected growth parameters of the child's cognitive, emotional, social and moral development. You need to cope with a growing and questioning mind, frequent social and emotional upheavals, and still do your best to bring up a well-adjusted child—the proposition is difficult but not impossible.

Children with learning disabilities, like other children, also have the same stages of development. However, their struggle is far greater and they require immense emotional support. In the next section we learn what we mean by *learning* and *learning disorders*. Both *learning* and *learning disorders* have numerous concepts.

SECTION II

Understanding Learning Disability

2
Learning Concepts

Learning is a treasure that will follow its owner everywhere.
–Chinese proverb

EVERY MOMENT IN our journey through life we learn
something. Learning is a continuous and never-ending process,
starting from infancy to adulthood and continuing into old age.
Learning includes how we sit, walk, talk and socialize. We learn
the alphabet, numbers, and mathematical and scientific concepts.
We learn about our ancestors, earlier civilizations, geographical
locations and symbols. We learn to translate book knowledge and
apply it to understand the world around us, and vice versa. In
short, we are always learning something all the time. Learning is a
life-long and perennial process. Thus, we can say that we are born
with the capacity to learn.

We observe the learning phenomena right from infancy, when
a baby learns to distinguish and use various senses like sight,
sound, touch, taste and smell. These senses then are differentiated

into meaningful activities like walking, talking and manipulating things. Basic motor, emotional, social and intellectual skills prepare an individual to step into and be accepted by society. Most children acquire these skills naturally at home. Once they step out of the house and into preschool, outside influences become equally important for their growth. It is formal schooling that is instrumental in shaping the child's psyche, personality and individualism.

What Is Learning?

Learning, as we understand it, is the ability to acquire knowledge and to be able to perform new behaviours based on that knowledge. Scientifically, learning can be defined as 'a relatively permanent change in behaviour that occurs as the result of prior experience', as per Hilgard et al.[1] Permanent changes also occur due to the growing up or maturation process. Both the concepts are closely linked. Learning cannot take place without the optimum development of the child. Even if you try teaching the child before the maturation level, the child will find it difficult to grasp the concept or, at the most, may grasp it partially.

To understand more about how learning takes place, we will talk about the laws that govern learning. These laws determine what is learnt, how much is learnt and what is retained of that learning.

The Laws of Learning

An eminent psychologist, Thorndike, gave three laws of learning, namely, Law of Readiness, Law of Exercise and Law of Effect.[2]

(a) Law of Readiness

This law relates to the degree of preparedness and eagerness to learn. Those individuals who learn the best are ready to learn and see the reason to learn. Conversely, it is equally true that those who are neither eager nor see a reason to learn will not learn.

(b) Law of Exercise or Law of Use and Disuse

This law states that the things that are most often repeated are best remembered, hence called Law of Use. Those learnings that are infrequently used or sporadically practised are weakened and forgotten easily, thus called Law of Disuse. It is well known that if something is repeated often one tends to remember it. The proverb 'Practice makes perfect' represents this law. Thus, practice of a taught task is a tool in the hands of educators to ensure that retention of the learnt material takes place.

On the other hand, if the learned skill is not exercised properly, it will soon be forgotten. This law is very effective in correcting inaccurate/incorrect actions. If a mistake in performance is corrected and the wrong response is not allowed to reoccur, then the incorrect response is soon forgotten. Here, the emphasis is on accuracy rather than on speed.

(c) Law of Effect

This law states that learning is strengthened when it is accompanied by a pleasant or satisfying feeling, and is weakened if associated with unpleasant feelings. Thus, the emotional state of the learner contributes to the learning process. It is felt that learnt material that is interesting and satisfies an inquisitive mind will naturally be repeated and remembered by a student. A word of praise by the teacher adds on the desire to learn, thereby making retention better. A student needs to experience success at the first learnt task to feel encouraged and motivated for further learning. Failure at the first task itself may act as a deterrent for the future learning process.

(d) Law of Exercise

Once the student is ready to learn, feels motivated to learn and has adequate tools to learn, the natural desire is to acquire and retain the new information or skill. To retain this new information, practicing exercises need to be done. Repeated practice ensures that learning does take place.

However, if a long gap is placed by the learner between each practice session, this increases forgetfulness. Practice alone is not the only factor for remembrance and recall. The other crucial factors are interest, motivation to learn and purpose to learn. When there is a sense of satisfaction or achievement, it enhances the desire to learn.

Thorndike's Eight Secondary Laws of Learning

The laws provided by Thorndike are as follows:[3]

1. **Law of Primacy:** This indicates that first impressions are the strongest impressions. Hence, learning needs to be correct the first time itself, as unlearning the wrong and relearning the right takes a longer period of time.

2. **Law of Recency:** This law emphasizes that the most recent learning is better remembered. Translating that to academics, it can be said that the text learnt the last would be most easily recalled while reproducing it. Hence, revision of the syllabus on the day prior to examination would be recalled with more clarity.

3. **Law of Intensity of Stimulus:** The stronger the intensity of the stimulus, the stronger is the response, and vice versa. An examination is a strong stimulus that inculcates

a strong response to prepare for it. An enthusiastic student would prepare and achieve more than an uninterested one.

4. **Law of Multiple Responses:** This law determines that in a novel situation an individual would give multiple responses to arrive at the correct solution.

5. **Law of Set Attitude:** The learner performs better if the attitude set is positive. In other words, the attitude to learn is present.

6. **Law of Analogy and Assimilation:** Learning takes place by comparison or analogy and assimilation. When the student can correlate the learnt material by finding similarities and dissimilarities, the recall is greater. The closer it is to the individual's experience, the more firmly it is embedded in the mind.

7. **Law of Associative Shifting:** This law describes how a learned response to one stimulus can help in responding to another similar stimulus. Simply put, it is the ability to associate a response to a new but similar stimulus. This is based on the trial-and-error method of learning.

8. **Law of Partial Activity:** This law states that the learner is able to respond to some specific aspects of the stimulus, rather than to the whole.

Factors Influencing Learning

A vast number of factors affect the learning process. Amongst the numerous factors, some play a more crucial role. These factors are age, intelligence, motivation and prior experience.

a) **Age:** Age is an important determinant in influencing the learning process. At every age, human beings have the capacity to learn, although as one starts growing old the speed and efficiency of learning slows down. The learning process also slows down if a person suffers from diseases like dementia, and, especially, Alzheimer's disease.

b) **Intelligence:** Since time immemorial it is well known that intelligence is an important determinant of the learning process. The difference in intellectual level affects what is learnt, how quickly it is learnt and what all is retained and reproduced on demand. Intelligence, although a frequently used word, has been difficult to conceptualize. According to Gardner,[4] intelligence has many different components like linguistics, logical–mathematical, musical, and interpersonal or social intelligence.

c) **Motivation:** Those persons who are motivated, learn much faster than those who are not motivated. At the same time, it has been seen that extreme cases—that is, too high or too low motivation—are both detrimental to the learning process. If a person is less motivated, then the chances of giving up a task soon is present. Too much motivation increases the likelihood of stress, which acts as a deterrent to learning because of emotional subjectivity. An optimal level of motivation is best suited to build a success story.

d) **Prior experience:** It has been seen that previous learning experience, especially of similar nature, helps in new learning. For example, if one has learnt to drive a car, it will be easier to handle other cars although the make and feel of the new car is different. This phenomenon is called *positive transfer*. On the other hand, sometimes the previous learnt experience acts as an impediment in the acquisition of a new response. For example, in cases where memorizing the first lesson hinders in memorizing the second, the process is called *negative transfer*. Negative transfer is often seen while trying to learn two similar languages. The one learnt first hinders the learning of the second.

Learning Basic Skills

Learning is a multi-dimensional and multi-modal phenomenon. We learn a lot many things in life but some basic functions that are imperative for our existence are language, observation skills, motor skills and concept formation.

Language Learning

Learning to master a language is one of the most difficult tasks. Yet, most human babies learn to speak and understand words and sentences in the first few years of their lives. Linguist Noam Chomsky indicated that human babies have an inbuilt capacity to acquire language.[5] This was supported by later research. Certain areas of the brain—like Wernicke's Area and Broca's Area—are involved in the process of learning the dynamics of language. When these areas are damaged, the person loses the ability to speak or comprehend language.

Observation Skills

Learning by observation is one of the most powerful tools. Right from the beginning, the child learns to observe and imitate parents, siblings, neighbours, teachers and persons living in their vicinity. Learning through written or spoken language, or hearing, is a variant of observational learning as it allows imitation or modelling of other people's experiences. Reading and any form of mass media are different ways of learning and communicating. In fact, virtual and e-learning are fast overtaking conventional school teaching.

Motor Skills

Motor skills provide the ability to perform a set of complicated but coordinated physical movements. For example, learning to eat, write, type, drive a vehicle, play a musical instrument, do sports activities, are all complex but coordinated motor skills. Once the relevant motor skills are learnt, the act is performed automatically, like driving a car or typing a letter.

Concept Formation

When a person can organize information into categories, they have learnt concept formation. For example, a child learning to identify banana, mango, pear as fruits despite difference in their shape, size and colour. As the human baby grows older many concepts are learnt—from simpler ones like animals, food, flowers, games and toys, to complex and abstract ones like peace, politics and ethics, as one progresses from childhood to adolescense and adulthood.

Although language facilitates concept formation, it is not the only important condition. Animals like chimpanzees, monkeys, birds too can learn simple concepts.

Explaining the Learning Phenomena

Based on a person's performance, one can determine if learning has taken place. However, it is not easy to understand the process through which learning takes place. Different scientists and psychologists have offered varied explanations. They have been categorized as: classical conditioning, instrumental conditioning and cognitive learning.

A) Classical Conditioning

Ivan P. Pavlov (1849–1936) first used this term while conducting experiments on dogs.[5] In these experiments he tried to gauge the relationship between the presentation of a *stimulus* and its subsequent response given by dogs. A stimulus is any object or situation that stimulates any one of the sense organs like sight, touch, smell or taste. The stimulus (S-1) generates a response (R-1), and the person learns the association between this stimulus and its corresponding response. In his experiments, Pavlov noticed that when food was presented to dogs they automatically salivated. This he termed as an unconditioned stimulus (food), which generates an unconditioned response (salivation).

He then paired the sound of the bell (neutral stimuli) with presentation of the food (unconditioned stimuli) to which the dog salivated (unconditioned response). After repeated pairings, the bell (neutral stimuli) brought about the salivation (conditioned response) in the dog. Later, Pavlov noticed that when the dog heard the lab assistant approaching (neutral object), the dog would salivate just by hearing the footsteps of the assistant as it had learnt to associate the presentation of food with the footsteps of the assistant.

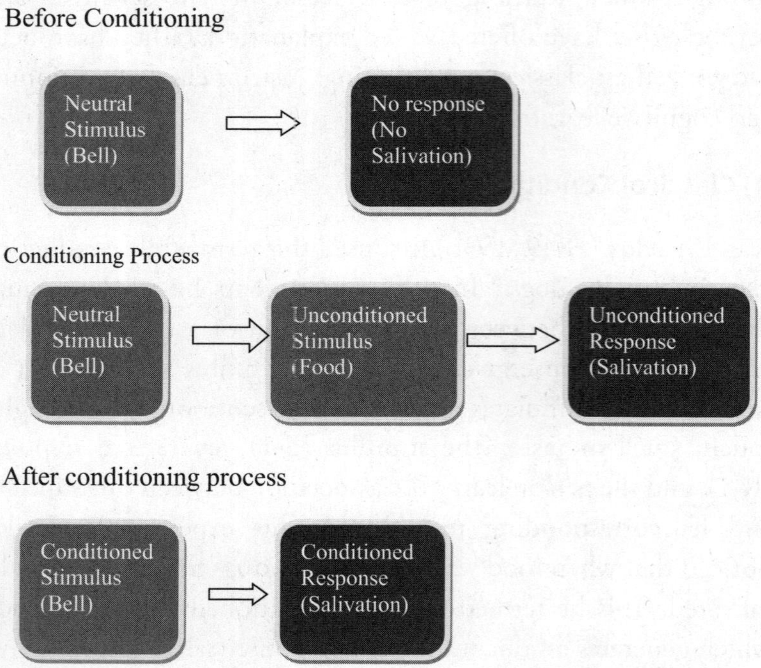

Before Conditioning

Neutral Stimulus (Bell) → No response (No Salivation)

Conditioning Process

Neutral Stimulus (Bell) → Unconditioned Stimulus (Food) → Unconditioned Response (Salivation)

After conditioning process

Conditioned Stimulus (Bell) → Conditioned Response (Salivation)

Figure 1: Classical Conditioning Theory of Learning

An example will illustrate this kind of learning theory. Young children, who are scolded often at school and at home for not studying, tend to view books with aversion. They have learnt to associate scolding (an unpleasant experience) with books (which *could have been* a pleasurable experience). Repeated association of this kind creates an aversion for any book in the mind of a child. The reverse is equally true. Pleasurable experiences enhance the learning process. Latter psychologists have criticized this theory as being too simplistic.

B) Instrumental Conditioning or Operant Conditioning

Eminent psychologist B.F. Skinner coined the term 'operant'.[7] It explains that the occurrence of behaviour is brought about when something 'operates on the environment'. In simpler terms, a person operates/manipulates the environment or does some action to gain a reward. When it is perceived that a reward has been achieved, then learning through association between the activity and reward takes place. Every time the individual gets a reward for performing the same/similar behaviour, a tendency occurs to repeat the behaviour. An example will illustrate this point better. If the teacher praises a child for good behaviour in the class, at least in front of the teacher, the child will strive to exhibit good behaviour even if it is only to project and protect a good image.

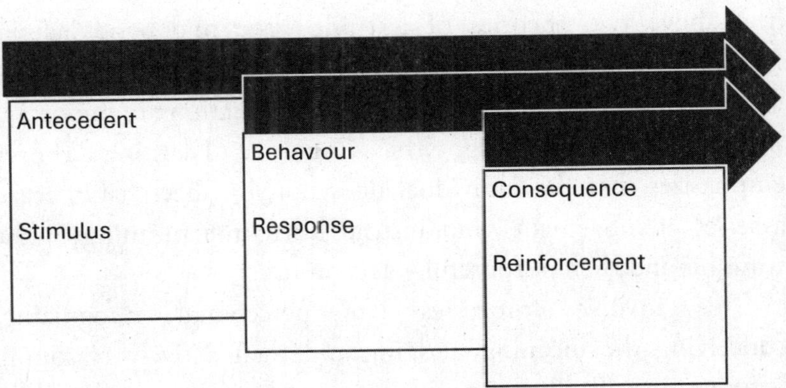

Figure 2: Operant Conditioning Theory of Learning

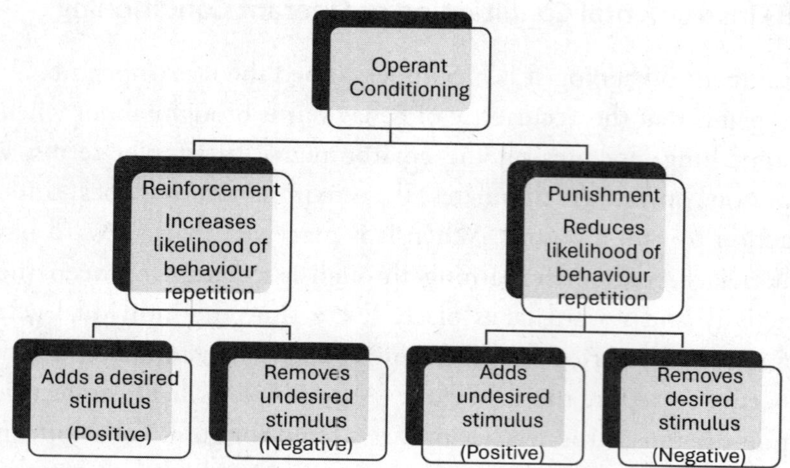

Figure 3: Effect of Reinforcement on Learning

C) Cognitive Learning

The above two theories of learning have one basic lacuna. Neither of the two take into consideration that one's thoughts and the meaning that one attributes to a situation are important ingredients for learning. The Cognitive Learning Theory emphasizes that the individual does not, by sheer habit, learn a series of movements, but instead learns the meaning of the stimulus and then purposefully acts on it.

This involves processes like perceiving, recognizing, conceiving the meaning, judging and then actively reasoning before acting. To illustrate with an example, if you watch a child putting together the pieces of a jigsaw puzzle, you will notice several things. Initially the child will try to fit a piece anyhow, but will soon realize that none of the pieces are fitting. He may then accidentally fit one piece with another. Subsequently, he will look for the shape and size of the piece and try to fit it or see which cues are leading to the correct solutions. Here you can see that active thought processes are at work and the child is using the insight method of solving the problem.

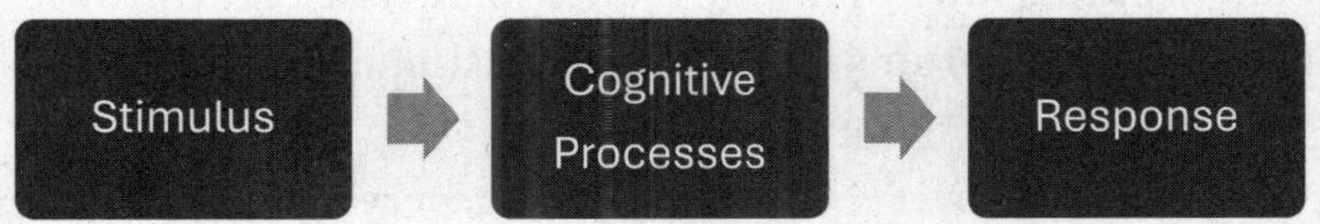

Figure 4: Cognitive Theory of Learning

Some Key Concepts

Generalization: Generalization in learning happens when past learning is used in mastering present learning. A person who learned to balance and ride a bicycle would be able to balance and drive a motorbike too. Generalization occurs also in situations where a person has faced unpleasantness. If a place or person is associated with unpleasant memories, the chances are that the person would avoid similar places or persons. To illustrate the point, a young lady was scolded at her workplace by an irate boss. She left that job and when in the next job she perceived her current boss as being like the previous one, she resigned despite no untoward occurrence. And after her marriage, she persuaded her husband to live separately from his parents as her mother-in-law reminded her of the boss. Clearly generalization had occurred in this case.

Discrimination: Discrimination learning is the ability to respond differently to different stimuli. Taking the above example, if the lady had learnt to discriminate that all irate persons would not scold her, she would not have had been without a job and would perhaps have lived with her parents-in-law.

Extinction: Extinction refers to behaviour that has been previously reinforced, when no longer reinforced, gradually stops occurring. A child who throws temper tantrums but finds that no one is paying attention, would after some time cease throwing tantrums. The tantrums would thus get extinguished.

Spontaneous recovery: Spontaneous recovery involves sudden display of a behaviour that was thought to be extinct. In the above example, if the child's temper tantrums were paid attention to again, the tantrums would be displayed in the same way as earlier. Another example is being able to ride a bicycle, despite not have ridden for scores of years.

Since learning continues throughout our lives and affects almost everything we do, including our success, a disability related to learning can be demoralizing and disquieting to both the affected child and the parents. But what really is learning disability or LD? Read on to understand it further.

3
Learning Disability

Bhupi

BHUPI WAS A 10-year-old boy studying in Class V in a public school in New Delhi and belonged to a family with a high socio-economic status. His father was a senior bank manager and mother a senior bureaucrat working with the Delhi Government. He came with complaints of more than two years of school refusal, inability to cope with classwork, deteriorating academic performance, being disruptive in class and often not completing his homework. He was being promoted to the next class each year under the education policy of not failing any student till Class V. This year was crucial for him because if he failed to perform, he would have to repeat Class V.

His notebooks showed that he was still reversing 'b' and 'd', 'p' and 'q', 'm' and 'w', and 'm' and 'n'. Often 'on' was written as 'no', and 'was' was written as 'saw'. 'The' was variously spelt as 'het' and 'hte'. He was mirror imaging 's' and 'c'. Numbers were also reversed, as 51 was written as 15, 96 as 69, and so on. Mirror imaging was seen in 3 and 5. His spellings were very poor. Although he understood the concepts orally, his written work was below class level, as well as not age-level, and what he wanted to say was never aptly put on paper. There were many grammatical errors and many sentences did not make sense.

The parents expressed their disappointment and concern over the child's declining academic performance. They took turns to teach the child every day, but whatever appeared to be learnt was promptly forgotten the next day. According to them the child was intellectually above average and was extremely creative. He would make flowers out of a straw, various animals from paper napkins and could draw very well. He was fond of cooking and often made snacks for the family. The snacks were served on a plate that was decorated differently every time, using various ingredients like sauce, ketchup, raw vegetables and fruits. On being asked what he aspired to be, he immediately said 'cook'.

An intelligence test and specific learning disability (SLD) tests were administered. The intelligence test showed an IQ of 125 which falls in the superior category. The SLD battery showed difficulty in reading, writing, mathematics and written composition. A diagnosis of 'primary learning disability' was made, and he was referred to the special educator for remediation classes.

Learning disability is not a single disorder, but a group of disorders. It affects the acquisition, retention, understanding, organization and use of both verbal and non-verbal information. The child faces difficulties in one or more specific areas of learning or school curriculum, despite having average or superior intelligence. Learning disability ranges in severity and invariably interferes with the acquisition and use of one or more of the following important skills:

a)   Oral language (listening, speaking, understanding);
b)   Reading (decoding, comprehension);

c) Written language (spelling, written expression); and

d) Mathematics (computation, problem solving).

It can also cause trouble in organizational skills, social perception and social interaction.

Understanding Learning Disabilities

The National Joint Committee on Learning Disabilities (1998) defined 'Learning Disability' as 'a heterogeneous group of disorders manifested by significant difficulties in the acquisition and use of listening, speaking, reading, writing, reasoning, or mathematical skills'.

Learning disability is a disorder in one or more basic psychological processes that involve understanding or use of language, both written and spoken. An LD manifests itself in the inability to listen, think, speak, read, write, spell or do mathematical calculations. Learning disabilities do not include those learning problems that may result primarily due to visual, hearing, or motor disabilities, intellectual disability and emotional disturbance, or due to environmental, economic or cultural deprivation/disadvantage. *In simple words, a child with average or even superior intelligence with no other physical, neurological, emotional and social problems finds it difficult to learn to read and write.*

Learning involves basic skills in the following four areas:

1) Reception of information;

2) Integration or organization of information;

3) Ability to retrieve information from the brain; and

4) Communication of retrieved information to others.

When any one of the above skills are affected, the child's learning can be seriously impaired. The most common problems are seen in the following functions:

i. Problem in auditory perceptual skills: inability to understand what we hear;

ii. Problem in visual perceptual skills: inability to understand what we see;

iii. Problem in processing speed: taking a longer time than normal, to process any information;

iv. Problem with organization: inability to store information in an orderly manner to be retrieved at will;

v. Problem with memory: difficulty in both short- and long-term memory;

vi. Problem with fine motor skills: inability to dexterously use fingers, particularly in writing legibly and copying;

vii. Problem with gross motor skills: inability to control large movements of the body while walking, running, playing, crawling;

viii. Problem with paying attention: inability to sustain attention for the required length of time to complete a task;

ix. Problem with abstraction: inability to interpret symbols and concepts; and

x. Problem with social competence: inability to have effective communication or interaction with others.

Types of Learning Disabilities

Learning disability is a hidden handicap. To diagnose LD correctly, a constellation of symptoms need to be present. The symptoms can be divided into three major categories:

1) Developmental speech and language disorders;

2) Academic skills disorders; and

3) Others (including disorders related to coordination and learning handicaps, not covered in the earlier categories).

Developmental Speech and Language Disorders

Developmental articulation disorder: Some children are unable to control the speed of their speech. They also face difficulty in learning to make speech sounds and hence tend to misarticulate the words. To illustrate with an example, 'story' maybe pronounced as 'thory', or 'rat' pronounced as 'wat'.

Developmental expressive language disorder: This disorder is characterized by an inability to express oneself in speech; use adequate number of words to complete sentences; answer simple questions; and use age-appropriate vocabulary.

Developmental receptive language disorder: In this disorder, the child is unable to make sense of certain sounds, words or sentences. To illustrate, when shown the image of a 'cot' and asked to point to the correct spelling, the child points to the word 'cat'; similarly, 'wall' for a ball, etc. Once I had a child who had come for testing and I asked him to write his name that he spelt correctly but crookedly. When I asked him to write 'I sat on my bed', bed was variously spelt as 'bad', 'bet' and 'bat'. All children do make similar mistakes, but over time these errors reduce on their own. Nevertheless, individuals with LD continue making the same mistakes even as adults. Since usage and understanding of speech are inter-related, most individuals have problems in both receptive and expressive speech.

Academic Skills Disorders

Developmental reading disorder: This disorder is better known as *dyslexia*. Reading disorders usually are visible from a young age, as the brain of a dyslexic person processes language differently from that of a non-dyslexic person. The dyslexic child will be seen to face problems in decoding words, will read slowly and hesitantly, have language-based difficulties like word-finding and pronunciation, and often has poor spellings.

Developmental writing disorder: This disorder is known as *dysgraphia*. The child finds it difficult to write even simple words, commits numerous spelling errors, has problems with vocabulary, grammar and in understanding the rules of writing. The child is often unable to express in writing what they can easily articulate.

Developmental arithmetic disorder: This disorder, called *dyscalculia*, is typified by difficulty in learning to count meaningfully, understanding cardinal and ordinal systems, using arithmetic operations like multiplication, division, addition and subtraction, and an inability to group objects. Associated problems could be in understanding visual and auditory symbols, using problem-solving steps and understanding the concept of quantity.

Some Co-current Disorders (including disorders related to coordination and learning handicaps)

Motor skills disorder or developmental coordination disorder: In this disorder, the child has poor motor coordination, which results in clumsy gait, inability to hold objects, frequent tripping over and falling, bumping into people or objects, and an inability to perform day-to-day activities with finesse.

Attention deficit and hyperactive disorder (ADHD): This is often present with Academics Skills Disorders. A substantial number of children have a short attention span, poor concentration, impulsivity and, sometimes, hyperactivity. The common characteristics would be fidgetiness, difficulty in remaining seated, getting easily distracted, attention not sustained to complete the task, shifting tasks without completing the earlier ones, inability to play quietly, excessive talking, frequently interrupting others, not wanting to listen and being engaged in physically dangerous activities. In case the child has attention problems, it is important to first treat that before any remediation is done for LD.

Early Signs of Learning Disability

Pre-schoolers

It has been reported by parents that children who later go on to be diagnosed with LD have been different since childhood, as compared to their siblings at that age. Their child was also different from other children of the same age. Children with LD have normal motor or physical, social, emotional and cognitive development. However, problems may be visible from early childhood vis-à-vis communication and language development. They may learn to speak later and hence development of conversation is delayed as compared to other children.

In some children *misarticulating* of words can be seen. Misarticulation can be of distortion, omission, substitution or addition of sounds. Distortion occurs when the sound is produced incorrectly without being omitted or replaced, as seen in lisping where sounds 's' becomes 'z' or 'th' becomes 'd'. Often 'sun' is pronounced as 'thun' and 'zipper' as 'thipper'. Omission occurs when a sound has been left out, as when 'cat' becomes 'ca' or 'spoon' as 'soon'. Substitution occurs when one sound is substituted for another, as seen in 'rabbit' becoming 'wabbit' or 'good' as 'dood'. Addition occurs when one or more sounds are added as 'black' becomes 'bahlack' or 'school' becomes 'isschoola'.

Some other characteristics seen are slow vocabulary growth, difficulty in finding the right word and pronouncing the words differently. For example, 'kitchen' may be pronounced as 'kimchem' and 'water' as 'woker'. Some children have trouble rhyming words. For example, they may have to struggle with the 'at' series, like learning cat, hat, bat and rat. Even rote learning would be slower in comparison to other children. They may struggle with learning numbers, alphabets, colours, shapes and days of the week, following instructions and route finding. Two sets of instructions, if given simultaneously, would be mixed up with neither followed.

Following a routine that involves the daily chores of getting up, going for morning ablutions, brushing teeth and taking a bath may be carried out in a confused order. The same instructions may have to be repeated every day, and, even then, neither are they seen to be followed nor does the child seem to remember them.

Another characteristic trait is of clumsiness in walking, picking, twisting, skipping or jumping. While playing they would break toys, unable to reassemble them or place them neatly in a row. This is indicative of poor development of fine motor skills. If you ask them to build a column with building blocks, they may only be able to place three or four blocks on top of the other, before the tower crumbles.

School-goers

When the child starts going to kindergarten and formal schooling begins, some other typical characteristics are observed. The child does not easily adapt to new surroundings and may take a longer time compared to other children to adjust to school routine. There may be awkwardness in the company of other children, because following instructions like 'eat', 'play' and 'run', or 'do you want...?', may not be clearly understood. Compared to others, learning even by rote takes a longer time as seen while reciting nursery rhythms. Due to lack of coordination, difficulty would be experienced in simultaneously reciting and acting the poem out. This poor coordination is often associated to being accident prone.

From kindergarten to Class I the curriculum focus is on phonetic sounds. These children find it difficult to connect the sounds with the letters. They make consistent reading and spelling errors. For example, ***letter reversals*** are seen, like 'b' is written as 'd', 'p' is written as '9' and 'q' is written as 'p'. ***Letter inversions*** are also seen, namely 'm' as 'w', and 'n' as 'u'. Likelihood of ***transposition of words*** as 'angel' as 'angle', 'left' as 'felt' and 'split' as 'spilt' may be present. ***Remembering the exact words*** may also be difficult although the synonym may be correct. For example, 'home' may become 'house' and 'desk' as 'table'.

Another troublesome area often seen is difficulty in understanding number sequences and mathematical signs like addition, subtraction, division and multiplication. Learning of tables, comprehension of time—especially minutes and seconds—and concepts involving numbers, may appear complex to them.

All these characteristics are adjudged as developmental delay till such time as Class II or III or 7+ years of age of the child. If there is persistence in these signs and symptoms, then formal testing for LD is warranted.

Prevalence in India

Compared to the Western world, the concept of LD in India is approximately five decades behind, which relegates it virtually to the infancy stage. One of the core reasons is that for long it was considered a problem firmly pertinent to the English-speaking countries, and since English was not the primary language in India, therefore the problem could not occur here. Later, other reasons were cited for LD presenting in children, such as overcrowded classrooms, an urban population-related problem, lack of awareness and deficiency in adequate data.

There is not much data still about the prevalence of LD in our country. A recent study (2022) spoke about the difficulty in identifying LD as the diversity in languages spoken and the disparity in socio-economic status in India are major deterrent factors.[2] The absence of standardized procedure (Shah et al., 2019)[3] and lack of uniformity of assessment tools (Kuriyan et al., 2019)[4] adds to the difficulties. However, an estimated prevalence of 2–19 per cent of children being diagnosed as learning disabled has been given based on the existing assessment tools. However, these tests only capture those children who are studying in the English medium schools which leaves out children of the vernacular schools (RCI n.d.).[5]

Thus, we see that though the figures give a large range, approximately 10 per cent school-going children do face some type of LD. The figures show the magnitude of the problem. However, even today children are quite often thought to be just lazy and inattentive. They are frequently punished at school as well as at home. The key to the solution lies in early diagnosis and timely remediation. It is, therefore, imperative for the parents and teachers to understand the child's problems and do something positive about it. If the child is only scolded and demeaned, instead of getting relevant and timely help the child will further develop associated psychological problems.

It has been aptly observed by Reid L. et al. that 'No other disabling condition affects so many people and yet has such a low public profile and low level of understanding as LD.'[6]

4
Types of Academic Skills Disorders

Dyslexia

Tia

'DOCTOR, I HATE everyone,' was the opening remark of a 9-year-old girl, Tia. She had a tear-stained face and was resisting her mother's restraining hand that was stopping her from running out of the waiting area attached to my chamber. A hard, resounding slap was delivered on her cheek by the mother, before anyone could react to these words. I had to intervene immediately to diffuse the crisis and asked the mother to let go of the child's hand. Hugging and reassuring her, I brought her inside the chamber. Having noticed that she was clutching a doll, I initiated conversation by talking about the doll. However, when I asked her why she had been brought to the hospital, she again reacted aggressively and tearfully said, 'I hate my mummy, papa, teacher, school, studies.' When asked whom she loved,

she said unhesitatingly, 'Neena didi.' Neena was the domestic help in her house.

During the interview the mother alleged that Tia was mentally dull. Despite being 9 years old, she still could not spell simple words. In fact, her spellings were atrocious. She was unable to recognize alphabets, would confuse 'b' and 'd', 'p' and '9'. She got the mathematical operations wrong and would often confuse numbers like 19 and 91. Her handwriting was ill-formed and illegible. Often, she was punished by being locked in the washroom by her mother, for repeatedly making the same mistakes.

The school was also punitive towards her, albeit differently. She was either shamed in front of the class for repeatedly making the same mistakes, or was sent to the headmistress for not completing her classwork or homework. Every alternate day her teachers would lodge complaints in the school almanac and the parents were sent for. Since both parents were working, it inconvenienced them to keep rushing to the school.

The mother further elaborated that every morning sending Tia to school was an uphill task. The child would complain of stomach-ache and vomit out her breakfast. She would cry all the way to the bus stop and would only stop after boarding the bus. Since there was incessant stomach-ache and vomiting, all types of investigations were done. The reports did not indicate any anomaly, which compelled the parents to conclude that these were excuses being made for not going to school. Each morning, it was the duty of the father to see that she boarded the bus. This was accomplished by dragging the loudly crying child till the bus stop, and then literally pushing her inside the bus. Anger and frustration were writ large on the mother's face as she was being interviewed. The LD evaluation confirmed that the child had dyslexia.

What Is Dyslexia?

The word 'dyslexia' can be broken into 'dys' meaning inadequate, and 'lexia' meaning verbal language. It, thereby, indicates that it is a language-based disorder where the child finds difficulty in decoding single words. This difficulty is noticed despite the child having average (normal) intelligence, adequate schooling, environmental support (literate parents, not first-generation literacy) and without any hearing, visual and neurological impairment or difficulty. The term 'dyslexia' is used if the problem significantly interferes with academic and daily activities pertaining to reading skills. Dyslexia has been known by other names such as reading backwardness, specific reading disability and developmental word blindness.

Two major difficulties are seen in dyslexia—language processing and visual processing. Language processing problem is related to difficulty in phonological processing, that is, in manipulation of sounds. The person also experiences impediment in visual–verbal responses and spellings. The British Dyslexia Association has defined dyslexia as 'a learning difficulty that primarily affects the skills involved in accurate and fluent word reading and spellings'. It is distinguished by 'difficulty in phonological awareness, verbal memory and verbal processing speed'. Hence, it is sometimes also known as developmental dyslexia.

Brain damage due to accident, injury, stroke or atrophy too can lead to learning difficulties. This is different from dyslexia, as it is an acquired learning difficulty. Hence the name *acquired dyslexia* or *alexia*. There are many types of alexia, namely *pure alexia, surface alexia, semantic alexia, phonological alexia* and *deep alexia*.

Typical Signs of Dyslexia

Dyslexia has certain characteristic features. One or more such features may be present:

i. Reversal of letter or words while reading;

ii. Reversal of letters while writing;

iii. Reversal of letters or words while orally reciting;

iv. Poor reading comprehension, though listening comprehension may be adequate;

v. Reading often being slow and laborious;

vi. Punctuations ignored while reading and writing;

vii. Difficulty in understanding, remembering and reproducing what has been read;

viii. Small functional words like 'is', 'the', often misread, omitted or substituted;

ix. Lack of awareness of the use of phonemes, i.e., the smallest unit of spoken language, for example 'bed' maybe variously pronounced as 'bad', 'bet', 'bag';

x. Often have difficulty in remembering instructions;

xi. Have difficulty in expressing themselves while writing;

xii. Handwriting and sometimes drawing/sketching are poor;

xiii. Numerous erroneous spellings;

xiv. Problems in reading new words. Few children use 'word attack' skills that enable them to break the words into smaller words and create an understanding for themselves. For example, the word 'waterfall' may be a new word but by breaking it into 'water' and 'fall', the child understands it. Similarly, other words like 'understanding' can be broken down as 'under', 'stand' and 'ing'. Thus, breaking them into familiar words helps to make sense of the word; and

xv. Clumsy, awkward and ungainly body movements suggesting poor body coordination and balance, making functions like walking, hopping, jumping, skipping, tying shoelaces and buttoning effortful and difficult.

Dyslexia in Adolescents and Adults

Dyslexia is a lifelong problem. Despite remediation, some symptoms may persist in adolescence and adulthood. Those with dyslexia continue to struggle to organize themselves, whether in personal or work life. One continues to see them with an unkempt appearance, shirts being wrongly buttoned or shoelaces undone.

Similarly, their written work is untidy and badly organized. Despite being well-versed in their subject, they may not be able to express themselves adequately and in an organized manner. Most dyslexics need to make an effort where sequencing of ideas is required—such as in a composition, letter, essay, report or story. Often, one sees them struggle to meet deadlines, as they are unable to classify work in a systematic order.

Their ability to copy from the board or even from a textbook may remain impaired, and they may continue to skip words and lines. Remembering numbers, particularly telephone numbers and PIN numbers of bank cards, may be tough for them. This is more so when dyscalculia is present. Often dyslexics complain of their cards being blocked, as they would have reversed the digits while feeding in the PIN number.

Spellings remain a lifelong problem. With constant use, common words are spelt correctly, but unfamiliar and difficult words continue to be misspelt.

Frequency of Occurrence

As per Sadock et al. (eds), about 4–8 per cent of the population in USA seem to have LD, and 60–80 per cent of this 4–8 per cent have a reading disorder.[1] The disorder is more common amongst boys. Signs of dyslexia become apparent by 6 or 7 years of age, when the child is in Class II or III. Diagnosing at that age would benefit the child the most, as remediation teaching can be started as early as possible.

	Word-level	Sentence-level
Normal reader	bed	He is lying on the bed
	book	She likes to read a book
Dyslexia reader	deb	He is lying on the deb
	dook	She lieke to reab a dook

Figure 5: Specimen of dyslexia (reading disability)

What Causes Dyslexia?

Extensive research on dyslexia has been carried out, yet **no** theory fully explains it. Research, however, has given certain pointers that clarify dyslexia. They are as follows:

Dyslexia is a *genetic* condition, i.e., children with dyslexia have family member/s with dyslexia. The gene on the short arm of Chromosome 6 is said to play an important role in developing dyslexia.

A *positive relationship* exists between dyslexia and cerebral palsy, epilepsy, malnutrition, difficult pregnancy and delivery accidents, use of tobacco and drugs by the mother during pregnancy and low birth weight of the child. These conditions are said to be contributory factors of dyslexia.

'Handedness', that is whether a person is right-handed or left-handed, was considered another significant factor. Since handedness depends upon which side of the brain is more developed, it was seen that children with dyslexia had a more developed right hemisphere making them left-handed. Hence a positive correlation between dyslexia and left-handedness, left-eyedness (predominant use of the left eye) and mixed laterality (using both right and left hand) have been found. Although later studies did not support these findings, it is well known that dyslexics confuse between left and right.

A possible explanation offered has been that the more developed right hemisphere of the brain has to take over the language functions of the left hemisphere and this leads to cerebral asymmetry—lack of balance of brain functioning. Hence, there is confusion in the brain of the dyslexic that results in reading difficulties. However, since their right hemisphere is more developed, such persons are good artists, musicians, athletes and have unusual mechanical and 3-D visualization ability (the ability to perceive length, breadth and depth).

Dyslexics have unique brain architecture and have **unusual neuronal wiring**. Neurons are found in different parts of the brain as compared to non-dyslexics and the brain structure is not as neatly ordered.

Imaging techniques like MRIs have shown that the dyslexics neither use the same part of the brain as non-dyslexics, nor are they consistent in the use of the part of the brain while reading.

Dyscalculia

Vidhu

I was summoned to the Intensive Care Unit (ICU) to counsel Vidhu, a young girl of 12 years, who had severe stomach cramps with no apparent medical reasons. All her pathological reports were within normal range and endoscopy too did not show any anomaly. Since there was no obvious reason for the cramps it was felt that psychological analysis may uncover some rationale for the pain. The child appeared anxious but not depressed. On mental status examination she acknowledged being tense, but was evasive in answering questions. She surprisingly showed no interest in wanting to go back home. When psychological tests were administered, she showed severe anxiety and stress related to examinations and the school's periodic tests. However, the mother was not too keen for further assessment and since the pain had subsided the child was discharged.

A month later I again got urgent summons from the ICU. The child was back with almost identical symptoms. A battery of pathological and radiological tests again did not reveal any apparent medical reason for the pain. This time I interviewed the mother independently. Trying to gauge the precipitating factor that led to stomach pain, the mother lamented that due to abdominal pain the child had missed her second mathematics test. She was doubtful whether the child would be able to score well in her half-yearly examinations and pass the subject. Further probing revealed that the child had been doing poorly in mathematics since the beginning. It had been an uphill task for the mother to teach her basic concepts, such as what came before a number and what came after, writing numbers in thousands and lakhs, identifying bigger and smaller numbers, and so on. Vidhu would confuse numbers and write them in reverse, 16 was written as 61, 39 as 93. Historically, mirror imaging was present particularly for numbers 3, 5 and 9.

It was a stupendous task for me to convince the mother that it would be beneficial to assess the child for LD. The LD battery strongly indicated dyscalculia. Her grade level was of Class II and she was then studying in Class VII. However, the mother did not accept the findings of the LD battery and the child was discharged.

A third admission in the hospital happened a month later, during the child's half-yearly examination. This time the child's father requested the ICU team for psychological intervention. When he was shown the protocol of the test administered a month ago, he appeared convinced that the child did suffer from dyscalculia. A formal report of the test findings was given to the parents to be submitted to the school. However, the report was not submitted and with every cycle of tests, a fresh admission to the hospital was made with identical symptoms.

At this juncture, the school counsellor contacted me to discuss the repeated admissions to the hospital and whether the failure of the child in mathematics tests was confirming the presence of dyscalculia. A meeting was arranged between the parents, school authorities and I, where the performance on the tests, class notebooks and LD test findings were discussed. It was decided that the child be allowed to discontinue mathematics and in lieu take up another subject, computer application. Henceforth, the child was not seen again in the hospital.

'Dyscalculia', with 'dys' meaning inadequate and 'calculia' connoting calculation, means difficulty in computation. A person with dyscalculia would have difficulty in understanding, learning and comprehending mathematical concepts. This diagnosis is made when the intelligence is average or above average and there is no history of any brain damage or insult, either by injury, disease or seizures. In case of brain insult, it is referred to as acalculia. Dyscalculia has been variously described

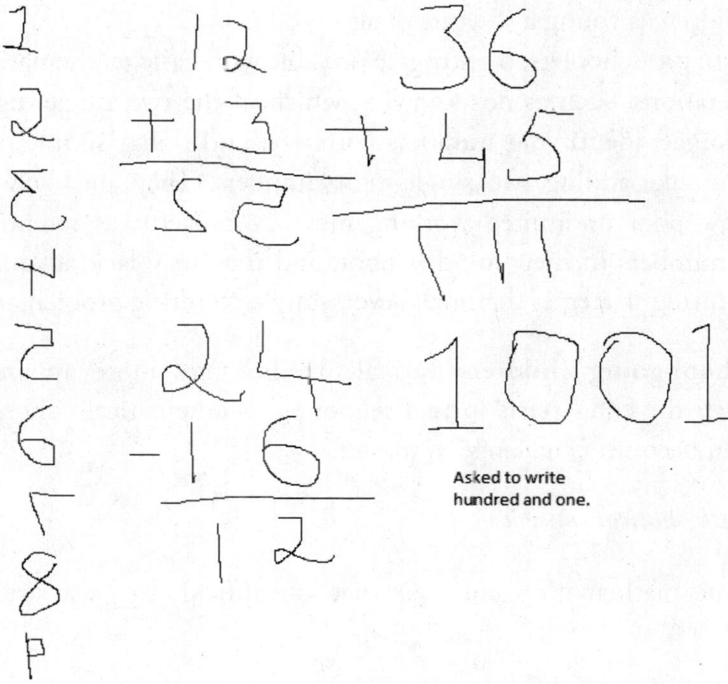

Figure 6: Specimen of dyscalculia (mathematical disability)

as *Developmental Dyscalculia, Mathematics Learning Disability, Mathematical Learning Difficulty, Mathematical Disability, Arithmetic-related Learning Disabilities, Arithmetic Disability* and *Arithmetic Learning Disability*. Dyscalculia is innate, genetic or developmental in its origin.

Typical Signs of Dyscalculia

Pre-schoolers: Dyscalculia is often visible from a young age. Compared to other children of the same age, children with dyscalculia would have difficulty in knowing how many items lie within the visual subitizing (rapid, accurate and confident judgments of numbers) range. Subitizing ability is present in children as young as 5 years of age.

In pre-schoolers, the struggle is visible with basic mathematical operations, such as not knowing which of the two single digits is larger; identifying numbers correctly; and doing simple oral sums like adding two single-digit numbers. They are likely to show poor or limited working memory capacity, as retention of numbers in their mind is poor, and they may lack adequate counting strategies that make even simple counting problematic.

School-going children: Dyscalculia becomes more apparent when the child starts formal schooling. Mathematical concepts then become a challenge to master.

Mathematical concepts:

Some mathematical concepts that are difficult to grasp are as follows:

i.   Mathematical operations like addition, subtraction, division and multiplication. The last two are the most difficult for them to understand, particularly division.

ii. There is a genuine lack of understanding of mathematical terms, as multiplication being repeated addition and division being repeated subtraction.

iii. Fractions, integers and decimals, simple unitary and ratio method would be hard for them to understand.

iv. Higher mathematical concepts are exceedingly tough for them, particularly geometry, algebra, logarithms, trigonometry and basic calculus.

v.   The ability to pick the salient facts from statement sums may be inadequately developed. So the child may not be able to judge which operation is to be used.

vi. Often, they tend to confuse printed signs and symbols.

vii. Reversal of numbers is seen so that 14 would be read as 41, and 39 as 93.

Time, distance and shapes:

i. The child would find it difficult to understand the concept of time. Hence, they would have problems in reading an analog clock.

ii. The concept of quarter (15 minutes), half hour (30 minutes) and three-quarters of an hour (45 minutes) would be a struggle to comprehend. Especially where the terms 'to' and 'past' are used. For example, 'quarter *to* nine' and 'quarter *past* nine' would often be reversely assumed.

iii. Reversing the hands of the clock and reading time too is problematic. For example, if the clock reads 10.25, the reverse time (2.35) would be difficult for them to calculate. Even oral calculations may be difficult for them.

iv. They have poor memory for retaining number information, like memorizing the tables, value of pi, formulas, etc.

v. They have poor visuo-spatial abilities and may find it tough to put the steps of a sum in an orderly fashion.

vi. Often when dyslexia is co-morbidly present, the child may have difficulty in reading the statement sums. As the comprehension of the statement sum is poor, it in turn confuses them about which mathematical operation to use.

Adolescents and adults: Dyscalculia persists in adolescence and adulthood as well. Such persons would have trouble in understanding Physics, Chemistry, Finances, Computer Sciences and Accountancy, and other fields that require mathematical skills. They would not be able to visualize the patterns involved, or gauge the relationship between concepts or components, and identify salient crucial information to solve equations or complex calculations. Even later in life, these people struggle while dealing with money transactions and managing their finances.

Frequency of occurrence: As per Sadock et al. (eds), dyscalculia alone, as a specific learning disorder, is seen in about 1 per cent of school-going children.[2] In other words, 1 in every 5 children, has the disability. The current prevalence range is estimated to be between 3.5–6.5 per cent, with the tilt in favour of girls being more susceptible to this disability. In fact, Sadock et al. (eds) conclude that dyscalculia is almost at par with dyslexia with regard to its occurrence.[3]

What Causes Dyscalculia?

Developmental perspective: There are many theories that have tried to explain this disability. Although none of them has been universally accepted as explaining the condition, nonetheless, at least some insight as to what causes it can be ascertained. In 1970, Ladislav Kosc proposed a definition of developmental dyscalculia:

> Developmental dyscalculia is a structural disorder of mathematical abilities which has its origin in a genetic or congenital disorder of those parts of the brain that are the direct anatomico-physiological substrate of the maturation of mathematical abilities adequate to age, without a simultaneous disorder of general mental functions.[4]

Kosc tried to separate primary dyscalculia from secondary dyscalculia. Primary dyscalculia has been defined as a mathematic deficit stemming from an impaired ability to acquire mathematical skills, whereas secondary dyscalculia or pseudo-dyscalculia is caused by external factors. Based on this distinction, many researchers—amongst them, Rubinstien and Henik—have distinguished primary dyscalculia as 'endogenous (having internal causes) LD'.[5] These researchers have also distinguished secondary dyscalculia as being a result of exogenous (external) factors like cognitive deficits that are not specific to numeral processing, such as working memory, attention span or visual-spatial processing.

Based on these theories, four commonly researched and experimented upon hypotheses were generated. The first hypothesis states that dyscalculia occurs due to *general cognitive deficits*. Briefly, it states that there is deficiency in cognitive skills to decipher numbers. The second hypothesis asserts that dyscalculia occurs due to a failure in the *development of specialized brain systems* that are required for processing of numbers. This hypothesis maintains that there are special areas in the brain meant for processing numbers that have remained undeveloped or underdeveloped.

The third hypothesis focuses on evaluating the deficit in accessing quantity representation through numerical or number symbols. In other words, a child suffering from dyscalculia is unable to connect the number symbols like 4 to the quantity 4. The fourth hypothesis emphasizes that dyscalculia is due to impairments in a *generalized magnitude system* that helps in processing continuous and discrete magnitudes. This hypothesis investigates whether the brain represents information from different magnitudes like time, space and quantity through a common mechanism. However, as stated earlier, none of these hypotheses have been unanimously accepted. In fact, more research is required to form a comprehensive cognitive model of numerical processing and its importance in disorders related to it.

Neuroimaging theories: One of the theories quoted most often is 'core magnitude representation' and it originates from the neurosciences. It is frequently also called the 'deficient number module deficit' theory. It explains that the number perception resides in the bilateral (both sides) intra-parietal sulci (IPS) of the brain. However, there is a gap between the structural abnormalities (brain abnormality) and functional (behavioural) aspects. It is prudent to point out that the IPS is involved in other significant functions vis-à-vis mathematics that are important for perception of numbers, like working memory, attention, spatial processing and inhibitory functions.

Piazza opines that dyscalculia occurs due to impairment in a cognitive system that humans use lifelong, called the Approximate Number System (ANS).[6] It furnishes an individual with the capacity to understand, estimate and even manipulate non-symbolic measures (those quantities that are not based on numbers as 1, 2, 3, and so on). This too was subsequently discarded.

Hence several working theories/hypotheses have been proposed. The importance of verbal and visuo-spatial working memory has been recognized in perception of numbers in many studies.[7] Verbal and visuo-spatial working memory have been found to be disturbed in dyscalculics. Parallel to visuo-spatial working memory is spatial processing, which too has been found to be deficient in dyscalculics.[8] Spatial processing is crucial for perception of numbers and mathematical computations as, without visualization of the operations involved, the mathematical operations would be difficult to perform along a mental number line.

The central executive system has been found to be impaired in dyscalculics. This system controls the central executive functions, which are important for controlling and coordinating information, and selecting and processing it. In case of disruption in such a function, there would obviously be difficulty in processing mathematical operations. Also, there is a link between development of mathematical abilities and *inhibitory functions*. When inhibitory functions are underdeveloped, the chances of dyscalculia are high. Inhibitory functions indicate suppression of irrelevant information, which includes discounting the previous incoming information in the working memory, thereby changing the mental set.

Thus, three factors have been recognized as affecting the central executive functions: (i) inhibition; (ii) mental set; and, (iii) information flowing and updating in the working memory.[9]

Research is still being carried out to fathom the riddle of what causes dyscalculia. Earlier investigations have indicated that perhaps there is not a single, but multiple inter-related and inter-dependent reasons.

Dysgraphia

Dysgraphia—'dys' meaning inadequate or defective and 'graphia' denoting writing skills—is a deficiency in writing skills. Dysgraphia, therefore, symbolizes inadequacy in transcription which includes skills in handwriting, typing, spellings, orthographic coding and finger sequencing (the movement of muscles used for writing). Primarily, it can be said that there is disturbance in the written expression. The term dysgraphia also encompasses handwriting difficulty. Thus, dysgraphia denotes deficiency in both writing and handwriting skills. Dysgraphia should not be confused with agraphia, which is the loss of the ability to write due to brain insult, stroke or progressive degenerative diseases of the brain like dementia.

Writing is a two-phase process. The first is the linguistic phase that involves encoding of visual and auditory information into symbols that represent written alphabets or letters. The second phase is the motor phase, where actual writing takes place. Writing involves fine motor skills that seem to be impaired in those with dysgraphia. However, it is not necessary that all fine motor skills are impaired.

Writing involves the knowledge of letter sounds, i.e., the awareness of the letters or group of letters that represent the *individual* speech sound of language. In written language these speech sounds are called *graphemes* and in spoken language they are known as *phonemes*.

The ability to write therefore depends upon the learning of phonics. Phonics gives an individual the skills to hear, identify and manipulate phonemes to be able to collate the sounds to form words and the corresponding spelling patterns—the graphemes—to represent them.[10]

Types of Dysgraphia

There are essentially five types of dysgraphia, namely motor, spatial, phonological, lexical and dyslexic dysgraphia. Often the sufferer is seen to have more than one type. Let us understand each type.

Motor dysgraphia: The ability to hold the pencil correctly is impaired. The child either holds the pencil exceptionally tight, or in an odd manner so that writing becomes difficult. Their writing is mostly illegible.

Spatial dysgraphia: The child shows difficulty in understanding the concept of space. The child may be unable to sit the letters on the ruled lines, have trouble in spacing words, so that it would seem as if words were running into each other. Naturally, their writing is illegible, though such children make fewer spelling mistakes.

Phonological dysgraphia: Children have difficulty in spelling unfamiliar, non-words and phonetically irregular words. The struggle lies in remembering phonemes and where exactly to use them. The exertion is most in words where the similar sounding phonemes are present, such as 'c', 's' and 'z'.

Lexical dysgraphia: This is a less often occurring phenomenon. Here the child finds it difficult to spell irregular or unusual words, while regular words are spelt correctly. They seems to depend more upon standard sound-to-letter patterns, like spelling 'cough' as 'coff', 'light' as 'lite'.

Dyslexic dysgraphia: Though the children can copy well, in spontaneous writing they find it difficult to translate thoughts into written words, make many spelling mistakes and have a disorganized and an illegible hand, particularly in spontaneous handwriting. Though their fine motor skills seem adequate, the connection between thought and written expression appears compromised.

Priyanka

A 10-year-old child, Priyanka, studying in Class V, was referred by the school for assessment of LD as she was refusing to write in class. She came with her mother in brightly coloured clothes, with a stylish purse and fancy boots. She appeared to be a talkative child and kept interrupting while the mother was telling me the reason for the hospital visit. As the mother was hesitating in front of the child to give the family history, the child was requested to be seated in another room and some sheets, pencils and crayons were provided to amuse her.

The mother then revealed that she had been separated from her husband for a year and had come to her hometown. Both mother and child were living in a rented apartment and the maternal grandparents also resided nearby. She had emotional and financial support from her parents and a sister. Both the patient and her mother had had a horrendous time with the father, as he was alcohol dependent. The child had been exposed to regular verbal and physical violence at home. The reason why the mother had not separated earlier was that her in-laws were supportive and protective towards them, though were helpless to prevent the aggression. However, since their death, the situation had worsened, and domestic violence had increased.

The child had refused to write from the beginning of her schooling. Since the teachers knew the family background, they were sympathetic towards her, and she was not compelled to write. However, once she got to Class II, the demand to write increased. She started finding excuses for not writing in the class. This brought on scolding from the teachers. She would often complain of pain and fatigue while writing in the school or at home. In fact, her teachers and mother scolded her for sitting in an odd, huddled posture which was considered as the reason for the complaints of pain. This was taken as an excuse for not wanting to write.

She underwent IQ and LD tests. She was found to have superior intelligence, with an IQ of 122. The SLD battery indicated that she was several grades higher than her grade in Reading, Spelling, Comprehension and Mathematics. However, she had done very poorly on Composition writing and testing for writing skills. Her writing was illegible and rules of writing were still not learnt. For example, proper nouns were written in small letters, punctuations arbitrarily used, words knocked into each other as spacing was poor, and her speed of writing was exceptionally slow. Throughout the test, she complained of muscular fatigue at the back of her hand. She was diagnosed as having dysgraphia. What was earlier thought to be an emotional disturbance due to her circumstances, later turned out to be an LD.

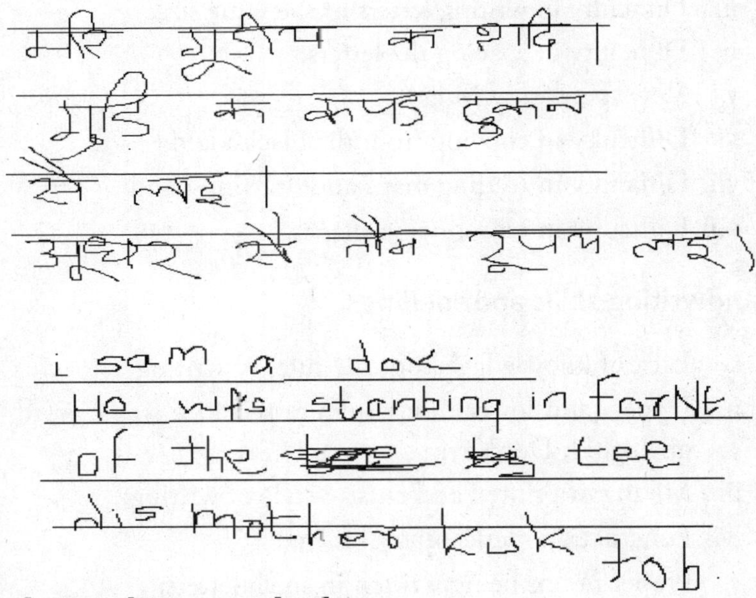

Figure 7: Specimen of dysgraphia (writing disability) with dyslexia (reading disability)

Typical Signs of Dysgraphia

One of the hallmarks of dysgraphia is messy handwriting. Messy primarily constitutes ill-formed letters, many scratched-out words, crabbed and illegible handwriting. Other signs and symptoms can be sub-divided as follows:

Visual-spatial difficulties:

i. Difficulty in sitting the letters on the ruled lines;
ii. Difficulty in writing in a straight line;
iii. Difficulty in writing letters of the same size;
iv. Difficulty in spacing the letters;
v. Slow speed of writing;
vi. Difficulty in copying from the blackboard;
vii. Difficulty in reading maps and drawings; and
viii. Difficulty in reproducing shapes.

Handwriting skills and spellings:

i. Lack of knowledge about the rules of writing;
ii. Upper- and lower-case letters mixed in a single word—giRl, goD, DonKey;
iii. Mixing of printed and cursive style of writing;
iv. Punctuation marks often missing;
v. Proper nouns being written in small letters;
vi. Making reversals, such as confusing between 'b' and 'd', 'p' and '9' or 'q', 's' and 'z';
vii. Hesitant while writing, as imagining the letter formation beforehand is poor;
viii. Prompting is required to make them remember the formation of the (particular) letter of the alphabet;

ix. Likelihood of excessive use of eraser;

x. Many spelling errors;

xi. An idea may be clear, but the same thoughts remain obscure on paper. Tandem use of thinking and writing, not seen; and

xii. Frequently, there is a complete refusal to write.

Fine Motor Coordination:

i. Pencil or pen is held very tightly, and the pressure exerted is more than required;

ii. Sitting posture is odd, leading to complaints of pain and fatigue in the muscles of the hand while writing;

iii. Finer motor skills are poor and this is seen in the way scissors, crayons, pencils and pens are held; and

iv. Difficulty in colouring and painting is seen, as the child is unable to colour within the margins.

Development of Dysgraphia through Childhood, Adolescence and Adulthood

Writing difficulty may be visible from early childhood when the child is initiated into scribbling, colouring and writing. An unusually tight grip on the pencil or colours is observable, with an odd posture of sitting while attempting to write. A reluctance to write or even hold a pencil or crayon may be present—including, as seen in the case above, frequent complaints of fatigue in the hand. The ability to space letters, sit the letters on the line and inability to follow the rules of writing are discernible from an early age.

As the child grows up, writing becomes more illegible. The child still may not have learnt the rules of writing and may not distinguish between upper- and lower-case letters. Since writing is so stressful for them, the concentration required to write may be so much that they fail to comprehend the meaning of the sentence. Often one can observe them saying the words aloud. Copying from the board or completing their classwork gets seriously compromised.

During their teen years, and even in adulthood, their struggle to express on paper is clearly visible. The thoughts in the mind do not match the written word. Often grammatical and syntax structure errors are pervasively present.

Frequency of Occurrence

There is a dearth of studies on dysgraphia and the few studies that are present are mostly in collusion with conditions like ADHD and autism. Hence, there is no consensus about the prevalence of dysgraphia. It is estimated that 5–20 per cent of all students have writing deficit.[11] Overvelde and Hulstijn studied students in Grades 2 and 3 and found that prevalence of dysgraphia ranged from 5–33 per cent.[12] Sadock, Sadock and Ruiz have given the range as being between 5–15 per cent.[13] According to them, it tends to reduce by youth. There are very few Indian studies on prevalence of learning disabilities in general and dysgraphia in particular. Mogasale et al. found 12.5 per cent of children with dysgraphia on a cross-sectional sample of children aged between 8–11 years from Classes III and IV.[14] The persistent rate of 4 per cent is seen in adulthood with the disability being more in favour of males than females, with a ratio of 2:1.

What Causes Dysgraphia?

Although no single theory satisfactorily explains dysgraphia, it is still thought to be a biological disorder indicating genetic and brain bases. It is primarily considered to be a working memory problem. As pointed out by J.M. Baldwin in 1896, since writing is a stratified process it implies that certain skills need to be developed before the child can write.[15] Some of these essential skills are the ability to sustain attention, development of language, short- and long-term memory, graphomotor skills, spatial ordering and sequential ordering.

Sustained attention: Attention needs to be sustained to not only speak a language but to write it too. Sustained attention is the ability to complete the task at hand without getting distracted or fatigued. This requires mental energy and persistent focus, so as to be able to keep track of the thought that needs to be committed in written form.

Language: Ever since development of language has taken place, it constitutes our very survival. It encompasses the ability to recognize letters and letter sounds, the ability to assimilate these sounds into words, the ability to comprehend the words and thereby the sentences, and then to be able to speak or state the sentence and convey the meaning to others. Sentences should be grammatically correct for the communication to be comprehensible.

Memory: The ability to write depends upon both short- and long-term memory. The ability to engender ideas, a retained vocabulary sufficient to express those thoughts, prior knowledge, and spellings—all are required to be able to write.

Graphomotor skills: These are a combination of cognitive, perceptual and motor skills, which facilitate the ability to write. When graphomotor skills are inadequately developed, writing becomes difficult as there is a discrepancy between thoughts and their expression in writing. Also, as the neuromuscular system is involved in writing, the muscles of the fingers and hand should be amply developed to hold the pen or pencil and manoeuvre it on the paper to be able to write. Often children with dysgraphia do complain of fatigue in the hand while writing as the graphomotor skills are not fully developed.

Spatial ordering: This is the method of organization that indicates how something is located or spaced in a certain area. For example, while writing on a page, how is it located? Is it top to bottom, left to right, and so on. The emphasis is on the arrangement of letters, words, sentences and ultimately paragraphs on a page.

Sequential ordering: Forming or following in a logical order or sequence. In other words, processing words and sentences and placing them such that the meaning and ideas are conveyed logically.

In dysgraphia, the normal connections among different parts of the brain required to acquire writing skills are not fully developed. Hence persons with dysgraphia are not automatically able to remember the sequence of motor movements that necessitate the writing skill. To be more precise, the capability to remember the sequence of motor movements to write letters and words is poorly learnt. This indicates that the coordination between orthographic coding (set of rules for writing), orthographic loop (storing of words in the mind's eye) and graphomotor output (result of coordination between the fingers, hands and the executive function of the brain) is insufficiently developed. Thus, a disconnect is seen between the sequential ordering, spatial ordering, feedback from the eye and motor movements to write—leading to inadequate motor output. The output is poor handwriting.

Therefore, the many coordinated abilities needed to write are poorly integrated in persons with dysgraphia.

Dysorthographia (spelling disorder)

A condition that co-exists with dyslexia and dysgraphia is spelling difficulty, though these two conditions (dyslexia and dysgraphia) are not exclusive to spelling difficulty. A certain pattern of mistakes that gives an insight into the said condition includes:

i.   Reversal of letters (similar to dyslexia);

ii.   Reversal of words (similar to dyslexia);

iii. Mistakes in use of similar looking words (same as dyslexia);

iv.   Omission of letters—'smoke' is written as 'smok';

v.   Addition of letters—'oral' is written as 'orral' or 'oraal';

vi.   Spelling errors while copying from blackboard or open textbook;

vii. Missing some consonants altogether, for example, 'consonants' may be spelt as 'consonets', thereby missing the 'nant' completely;

viii. Interchange of consonants, although all consonants may be present—'penalty' maybe spelt as 'pelanety';

ix.   Marked use of erasers; and

x.   Marked scratching out of words.

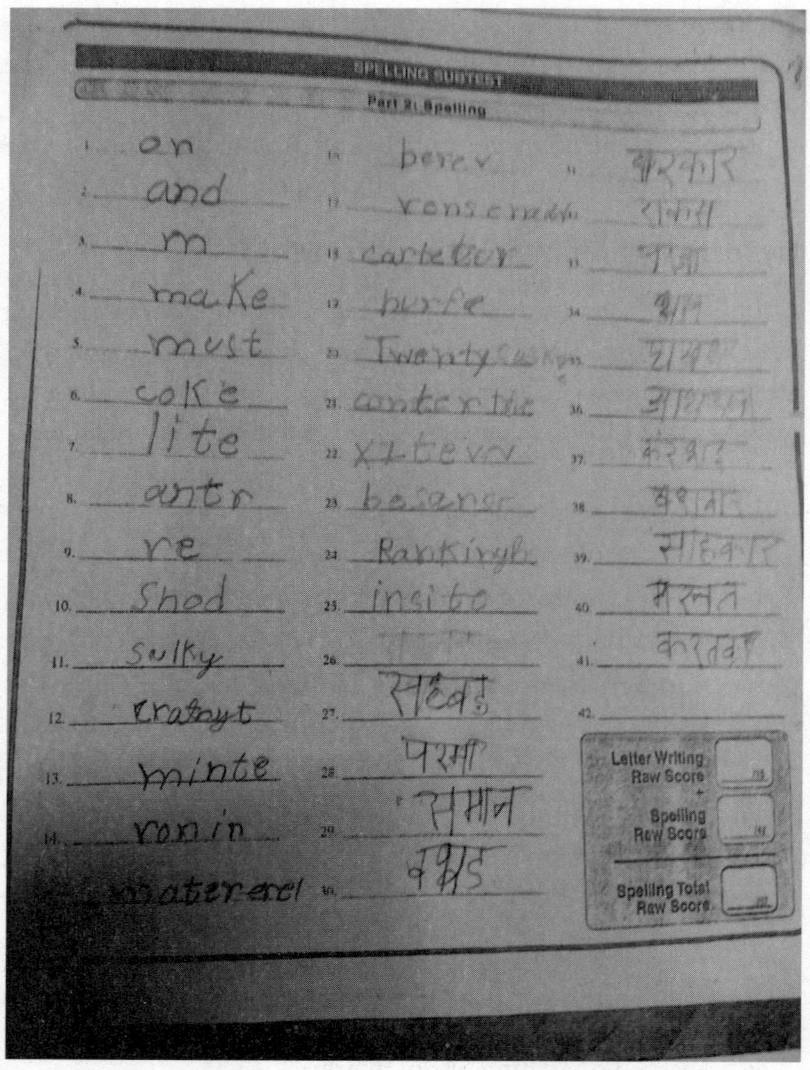

Figure 8: Specimen of Dysorthographia (spelling disability)

Simple words are wrongly written, for instance, 'cook' as 'coke', 'should' as 'shod', 'light' as 'lite', 'enter' as 'antr', and so on.

Frequency of Occurrence

Spelling errors are linked strongly to reading difficulty and vice versa. Children who are unable to spell, often flounder when they read and do not comprehend what they have read. Even when assessment to gauge LD is done, the composite score of reading, spelling and comprehension is taken into account, to be able to say with confidence that the child has an LD. Therefore, it is safe to say that in a large number of cases spelling problems co-exist with reading problems.

What Causes Spelling Errors?

Earlier it was believed that weak spellings (like a weak ability to read), was due to poor visual memory. Current thinking attributes it to inadequate language learning. As seen in reading and writing deficiencies, spellings too require a set of *cognitive functions* to be involved.

Letter formation is the first skill that needs to be acquired to write. Letter formation culminates when there is a coordination of fine motor skills with visual memory of the sequence involved in writing words. This is followed by *encoding* a word. In other words, encoding involves the ability to hear the sounds that make up the word and the symbols that denote it, that is, the alphabets/letters that form the word.

Short-term memory is required to remember the word as it is written. Thus, homophones, or words that are pronounced the same way but spelt differently, have to be remembered. For example, homophones like 'ate' and 'eight', 'blue' and 'blew', 'bye' and 'buy', and so on, have to be remembered by constant exposure while reading or writing. Consistent practice of writing leads to automatization of writing. As the child learns to write, the muscle movement involved in writing and visualization of the written word strengthens the spelling.

Later research indicated that spelling mistakes were not a result of poor visual memory, but like dyslexia, were due to difficulty in learning a language. Thus, as in dyslexia, spelling reversals are seen in 'b' and 'd', 'p' and '9', or reversals in the sequence of letters within the word, sometimes forming another word, e.g., 'saw' and 'was', 'stop' and 'pots', or in the sequence of phonemes within the word 'split' and 'spilt', 'bulk' and 'bluk', 'animal' and 'aminal' are usually present.

These mistakes indicate that the speller has difficulty in observing, remembering and subsequently recalling the letters involved in spelling the word correctly. Hence to write the spelling that approximately resembles the actual word, as well as remembering the phonemes, is not easy for such children.

Certain conditions like dyslexia, ADHD, dysgraphia and dyspraxia are also correlated to spelling difficulty. Thus, we see that many conditions determine the learning of spellings. Since learning of spellings like other academic skills is complex, one has to be vigilant as to the cause or constellation of causes, to be able to help the child.

Other Types of Learning Disabilities

The above-described conditions are considered as primary learning disabilities. However, motor skills (dyspraxia), language skills (dysphasia), and auditory and visual processing are other types of disabilities present concurrently with primary ones. Let us understand them in some more detail.

Dyspraxia: Affects Motor Skills

Dyspraxia is a motor dyscontrol disorder where the person has difficulty in muscle control, leading to problems in movement and coordination, and language and speech. It is not a learning disorder, but if present, it hampers learning. Dyspraxia may be seen alongside dyslexia, dyscalculia and ADHD.

Typical signs of dyspraxia:

i.   Child appears clumsy and frequently falls or bangs into objects.

ii.   Child has difficulty in coordinated movement.

iii. The child's eye-hand coordination is poor.

iv.   Child has inadequate motor planning.

v.   Fine motor skills are poor, so that from holding a pencil to activities like colouring within lines, joining pieces of puzzles, cutting pictures and pasting them, are all hard to accomplish.

vi.   Toys may often be broken and the child has poor skills to piece them together.

vii. The child has problems in organizing articles, so has a disorganized cupboard, torn and tattered notebooks and books.

viii. The child lacks neatness in appearance and in placing objects around themselves.

ix.   Some children may display excessive sensitivity to touch and hearing. Sensitivity to touch may include reacting poorly to scratchy, heavy, tight and rough textures.

x.   Auditory sensitivity may involve being troubled by sudden loud noises, or constant noise like the ticking of a clock, or a grating noise like writing with chalk on the blackboard.

Dysphasia: Affects Language Learning and Use

Dysphasia is a language disorder marked by deficiency in generation and comprehension of speech due to brain insult (injury). Language is an output activity as it requires the brain to organize thoughts and recall the correct words to express or communicate the thought to others. This requires two abilities to function simultaneously and complementary to each other. These are the ability to verbally speak, and to be able to comprehend the spoken word in order to communicate.

Thus, dysphasia is a speech disorder where the ability to express speech, signs, writing, comprehend spoken words and language gets compromised. There are three main types of dysphasia—expressive, receptive and global.

Expressive dysphasia: This is the most frequently occurring one. In this type, the ability to comprehend what is being communicated remains intact, but obstruction occurs in communicating one's own thoughts.

Receptive dysphasia: This occurs less commonly. It hinders the ability to comprehend and understand the language. Since language does not convey meaning to the person, their speech is characterized by nonsensical grammar, nonsense words and meaningless phrases. Thus, language may sound gibberish.

Global dysphasia: The is the severest form, where all language forms and skills may be disrupted.

Signs of Dysphasia

Some of the hallmark symptoms that characterize the dysphasic condition are as follows:

    i.   Difficulty in remembering and recalling common words;

    ii.   Difficulty in naming everyday usage objects;

iii. Difficulty in recalling names of even close family members;

iv. Inability to complete the sentence;

v. Speaking anyhow; thus the sentence may not make sense to the listener;

vi. Difficulty in reading and comprehending the read material;

vii. Difficulty in writing, as language does not make sense to them and hence they are unable to express language in its written form;

viii. Lack of lucidity of both expressed word and writing;

ix. Grammatical and syntactical errors;

x. Hindrance seen in expressing thoughts and emotions; and

xi. Difficulty in understanding spoken language.

Disorder in Auditory and Visual Processing

Auditory processing disorder, also called 'central auditory processing disorder', is when a person is not able to distinguish between the subtle sounds of words, even when the words are enunciated clearly and loudly. Many a times, the person may not be able to discern where the sound is coming from, or make sense of the phonemes present in the words, hence there is confusion in the order of the sound of the word. The ability to separate the background noise and block it to hear the word may not be present.

Typical signs of auditory processing disorder:

i. Difficulty in remembering verbal instructions, but accurately remembering non-verbal ones;

ii. May have difficulty in clearly explaining the ideas, as they appear jumbled and confused;

iii. May have difficulty in segregating similar sounding words like free/three, spit/split, lame/dame;

iv.   Misspellings are often present—'dress' could be written as 'tress', 'bad' as 'bed', and 'make' as 'shake';

v.   Mispronunciation—'spell' may be spoken as 'speel', 'felt' as 'left', and 'ceiling' as 'shelling';

vi.   Difficulty in understanding figurative language like metaphors, similes and puns especially related to pun jokes;

vii. May have comprehension difficulty in interpreting the nuances of the sentence, and will understand it literally;

viii. May have difficulty in evading the background noise to hear the sentences spoken;

ix.   May have a poor attention span, so that long conversations cannot be sustained or understood;

x.   Rapid or quickly spoken sentences may not be comprehended at all;

xi.   Often may ask 'what?', despite having heard the whole conversation reacts as if the sentence has not been comprehended; and

xii. When absorbed in activities, may not actually 'hear' a person talking to them.

Visual Processing Disorder

This disorder affects the person's ability to apprehend information that is visually seen. The problem is not due to vision or any anomaly with the eyes, but rather due to how the brain processes the information it receives. Shapes, letters, symbols and numbers are not easily differentiated. This disrupts the ability to understand the written symbols. Besides, gross and finer movement development may also be retarded.

Due to visual processing disorder, out of the eight issues possible, one or more types of visual processing issues may be present. The eight issues are: visual discrimination; visual figure-ground discrimination; visual-spatial; visual closure; visual sequencing; visual-motor planning; short- or long-term visual memory; and, letter and symbol reversal. Though visual processing disorder is often confused with dyslexia and even with conditions like ADHD, it is neither the same nor a similar condition. Visual processing disorder, like other learning disorders, is a lifelong condition and can be rectified somewhat by certain remediation techniques.

Typical signs of a visual processing disorder:

i.   Has confusion in recognition of letters, shapes and numbers;

ii. Problems are seen in identifying letters and words with certain sounds, or are reversed;

iii. Difficulty in copying from the blackboard;

iv. Mirror imaging is seen, as directionality of letters is tough to mitigate;

v.   Has problems in tracking the words and lines on a page while reading;

vi. Has difficulty in recollection of words, letters, symbols and numbers (including phone numbers) if exposed for a short duration;

vii. Since symbols are not easily remembered, mathematical equations become a challenge;

viii. Poor visual motor planning hinders handwriting, as recalling the alphabet and their directionality is not well remembered;

ix. Since visual processing is slow, the likelihood of poor attention span is present; and

x.   Spatial awareness is poorly developed, hence clumsiness is seen—as in running into or banging into obstacles like furniture.

OTHER ASSOCIATED CONDITIONS THAT IMPEDE LEARNING

Attention Deficit Hyperactive Disorder (ADHD)

This is a neuro-developmental disorder that is characterized by a short attention span and excessive motor movement or hyperactivity. The ADHD child has no regard for the outcome of such activity nor has fear of injury. The attention span and hyperactivity are both not in consonance with the age and development of the person.

This disorder may be co-morbidly present with LD. It is difficult to work with children with ADHD. They often lose pencils, papers, books, pencil boxes or even the water bottles they carry. Their parents report that their homework or classwork is seldom complete.

Inattention or poor attention span is typified by the following symptoms:

i.   A short attention span;

ii.   Difficulty in paying attention for sustained period of time to complete a task;

iii. Attention tends to fatigue quickly;

iv.   Is easily distractible and attention gets diverted;

v.   Unable to pay attention to details;

vi.   A tendency to lose things;

vii. Difficulty in organizing a task in a logical sequence;

viii. If the task on hand requires greater length of time to accomplish, the attention will waver much more; and

ix. A tendency to be forgetful in day-to-day tasks that may not require much effort.

When hyperactivity is also present, we see that:

i. Child is not able to sit for long;

ii. Squirms when seated or fidgets;

iii. Leaves the seat, even if specifically asked not to;

iv. Is unable to wait for his/her turn;

v. Indulges in high-risk behaviour, where knowledge of possible hurt is known;

vi. Appears to be always 'on the go' or 'driven by motor';

vii. Talks a lot, and is difficult to interrupt; and

viii. Tries to answer before even the question is completed.

One can empathize with the degree of struggle involved in learning what seems to come easily to others. Undoubtedly, this strife leaves an impact on the growing child's psyche, confidence, self-esteem, social interaction with peers and nearly all spheres of life. In my three decades of practice, I have come across innumerable children who came with other psychological disorders and were discovered to have LD as the primary condition. Let us see in what ways the child's mind and behaviour gets impacted.

5
Associated Disorders

'DOCTOR, I'M MAD, everyone says so,' was the opening statement of a 9-year-old girl studying in Class IV, from a family with a high socio-economic status. Although she walked in at a jaunty pace, her demeanour and facial expression showed distress. At that point I did not respond to the statement. Effort was made to make her feel comfortable enough to speak freely. After rapport was established, she talked about feeling lost and confused in the evening. The mother, who herself looked anxious, added here that the girl failed to recognize anyone, including the parents in the evening. She would become violent and hit them. Sometimes she would run out of the house and talk in a strange voice as if some 'ghost' had entered her body. In the altered state she would curse anyone who came near her and in particular, the mother. These episodes started after a month of her shifting from her home in the village to a city for better education.

These symptoms clearly pointed out to a psychological disorder called **dissociative disorder**, which usually occurs due to a strong psychological reason for a person to dissociate. Hence, psychological tests were administered to find the precipitating factor for her to dissociate. On a projective test, namely, Sentence Completion Test, it was seen that she was making typical errors that children with LD make. She was then tested for LD and was found to be positive for it.

Since she came from a rural background, she was being made fun of in class for her accent and general appearance. She blamed her mother for bringing her to the city, as she neither was able to adjust to the school nor cope with her studies. In the village she got her own way in most situations, as she belonged to a rich land-owner's family.

Although this is an extreme example of emotional disturbance in a young child, most children with LD do tend to have some kind of associated psychological problem. These disturbances may be inward directed or outward directed. In inward direction the feelings of the child are directed towards the self, as seen in depression, anxiety, lack of confidence, poor self-esteem and phobias. In outward direction the feelings are overtly expressed as aggression, temper tantrums and truancy.

In the above cited case, the feelings were mixed. The disturbance was indicating internal trauma, which she was unable to verbalize or speak about to anyone. She blamed her mother for taking her away from her comfort zone and putting her in dire situations, but she was unable to voice her feelings to her. As the mother was supportive and understanding, this made it doubly difficult for the child to express her anger towards her. So, it became a conflictual situation where her love for her mother conflicted with her anger towards her, and this anger was being expressed under dissociative state.

One of the commonest problems seen in children with LD is low self-esteem, poor self-concept and lack of confidence. The child may feel stupid, incompetent, timid and anxious. Self-esteem encompasses a belief in oneself. For example, the thoughts that 'I'm worthy', 'I'm competent' and 'I'm praiseworthy' are indicative of high self-esteem. On the other hand, when the thoughts are 'I'm useless', 'I'm good for nothing', or 'I'm a duffer', they point towards low self-esteem. Self-esteem determines how the child feels about self. Obviously negative evaluation of self will bring harmful repercussions.

Low **self-esteem** leads to poor development of self-concept. **Self-concept** is a collection of beliefs about oneself inclusive of academic performance, gender roles and racial identity amongst other things. Self-concept basically tries to answer the question, 'Who am I?' When both self-esteem and self-concept are lacking in a child, **self-confidence** too gets affected. Self-confidence represents the feeling of trust one has in one's own abilities, qualities and judgements. Imagine a child growing up with such negative self-evaluation. This would adversely affect the social, emotional, personal and educational adjustments, making it difficult to cope with simple problems in life, thereby, being riddled with self-doubt.

A little more serious problem seen in these children are anxiety-related disorders. **Anxiety** is an *apprehension* that something may go wrong. So, anxiety is intense fear, worry, or uneasiness that can last for long periods of time and significantly affect a child's life. Certain characteristic behaviours that indicate the presence of anxiety are complaints of headache, stomach-ache, backache, nausea, dizziness, inability to have sound sleep, nightmares, night terrors, and frequent stomach upsets and vomiting. Normally on pathological tests, the investigations may not reveal any pathology, thus affirming that these complaints are due to high anxiety.

One of the commonest anxiety disorders seen in children with LD is **phobia**. A phobia is an irrational fear. The children may show phobia for darkness, animals and closed places. A substantial number of them may have **school phobia**. School phobia is a slightly complex syndrome. It depends upon the child's temperament, and the circumstances prevailing at home and in school. School phobia may perhaps be inclusive of **separation anxiety**.

Separation anxiety disorder is when the child feels excessive anxiety when separated from parents, caregivers, siblings or a significant person in their lives. Autonomic symptoms may also be present as seen by dizzy spells, headache and stomach-ache. In a lesser form, the child may develop **school refusal**. This is easier to manage, as the child can be coaxed to school after speaking to the school authorities and listing their help. School phobia is more difficult to treat, as the child may not agree to even go near the gates of the school.

Severe anxiety can help develop another disorder called **obsessive compulsive disorder or OCD**. This is an anxiety disorder where unwanted thoughts or impulses repeatedly invade the mind of the child, compelling certain actions to be repeated to *relieve* anxiety caused by these thoughts. These obsessive thoughts cause *distress* as they are found to be foolish, frightening, disgusting, painful or trivial. Typically, the child tries to *ignore* or *suppress* each such thought or even tries to *neutralize* it with another thought or action. But despite trying to push the thoughts away from the mind the child is *unable* to do so.

Some of the common types of obsessions seen in OCD are thoughts of harm, contamination and doubt. The thoughts may range from the ideas of losing control, sinful thoughts against one's religion and fear of contamination. In adolescents, the fear of getting AIDS, harming someone, sexual images, counting and hoarding can be seen. Compulsions are behaviours that help relieve anxiety from these unwanted and intrusive thoughts. The child feels compelled to *do* something again and again so that the unwanted thoughts are somehow controlled. However, the repeated actions bring only temporary relief.

In most cases the child usually realizes that the repeated actions are *excessive* and *irrational*. Some common repetitive rituals are praying, washing and grooming, touching objects in a specific way, checking locks, light switches and gas, checking whether someone has been hurt by them, repeating certain actions like going through the doorway several times, counting objects like steps, hoarding items like old newspapers, scraps and used containers. The list is endless.

Impulse control disorder is another oft seen problem in children with LD. A variant of impulse control disorder is **trichotillomania**. In trichotillomania, the person pulls out hair from their head, eyebrows and eyelashes due to excessive anxiety.

A 15-year-old girl, Vineeta, studying in class X in a reputed public school of Delhi was brought to the hospital with the history of pulling her hair from the roots for the past two years. She had several patches of complete baldness. She appeared apprehensive and subdued. The history revealed that despite being a sincere student she continued to score poorly in academics. In the initial years of schooling, she had plenty of friends, but as she was promoted to higher classes, she started losing these friends. When she was in Class VIII, a group comprising her friends and classmates started teasing her mercilessly for poor grades. Even the teachers made fun of her in class. The essay she had submitted as homework was read out in the class and cited as 'How not to write an essay'. Henceforth, she was shunned by the class, and no one spoke to her or acted friendly.

The humiliation and anxiety related to academics increased multifold, and she started pulling her hair to relieve the anxiety. She was withdrawn from the school due to the hostile environment and admitted to another school by her parents. Despite being in a more friendly school, her hair-pulling did not stop. The worried parents then decided to bring her for consultation. The case history was suggestive of LD and the psychological tests substantiated it.

The most serious of all internalized disorders that one sees in children with LD, is **depression.** Childhood depression has certain marked features. Low and sad moods can be gauged from gaze aversion, labile mood (fluctuating from happiness to sadness in a short time span), prolonged visible unhappiness seen by sad expression and anhedonia (lack of pleasure from previously enjoyable activities). Despite attempts to make the child smile, one is likely to encounter only fleeting smiles to none at all. There is decreased social play and interaction with the peer group. The child socializes less and has withdrawn behaviour. Frequently, the wish to die, actual suicidal thoughts and suicidal attempts may be present. Depressive ruminations (thoughts) that lead to low self-esteem, guilt feelings, sense of worthlessness, helplessness and hopelessness are frequently part of their conversation. Some other persistent mood-related troubles seem to be increased irritability, frustration, temper tantrums and apathy. Often, they may complain of somatic pains like headaches, stomach-ache and backache. In young children, additionally, anxiety—especially separation anxiety—is present. Sleep and appetite are seriously compromised. *Depression in young children needs treatment and should not be neglected as inconsequential.*

A 13-year-old girl from Rajasthan, the only sister amongst three brothers, belonging to a rich and prestigious family, was brought to my clinic with fainting spells. These fainting spells had started about three months ago and she was already on anti-anxiety medicines. Since there was no improvement with medications, and the frequency and duration of fainting spells were increasing, the worried parents decided to seek a second opinion. On mental status examination the child appeared both anxious and depressed. Since no clear-cut precipitating factor was forthcoming, it was decided that psychological tests needed to be administered.

The tests threw up a plethora of information. The first and foremost was that she had typical LD signs, as seen in reversal of 'b' and 'd', very poor spellings, grammatical errors, and inability to form adequate sentences. The stories on Children Apperception Test seemed as if a child of primary classes had written them. The second equally important information generated was that she was actively contemplating suicide. In one of the stories the exact method to be used was described.

On further probing, it subsumed that she was finding academics difficult. Her family was not much bothered about her marks, as girls in their family were usually married early and only basic literacy was required. However, the girls in her school were ambitious and career-oriented and rather looked down upon her. No one actively teased or abused her, but slowly she was being marginalized in the class. The precipitating factor then emerged that a boy of her class said to her that she was good only for marriage. It shocked and distressed her so much that she fainted in class.

Subsequently this boy started to pay special attention to her in the class or during lunch break. Her name was frequently linked with his and they both became the talk of the class. She became fearful of being physically assaulted by him. She was also afraid that once her parents and brothers heard of her notoriety she could face severe consequences at home. All the three brothers were studying in the same school, with the eldest being in Class XII. When asked why she did not ask her eldest brother to speak to this boy, she replied that she was scared of being blamed for encouraging him. The circumstances were so stressful for her that it led to depression and suicidal thoughts.

Most children complain of **stress**. The word stress means a strain or push. Stress is often used interchangeably with other conditions like anxiety, conflict, ego-involvement, frustration, threat and excessive emotionality. Stress is a negative state that produces feelings of helplessness and inadequacy. Children perceive stress when they are unable to cope with the curriculum, punitive or hostile responses of the parents and teachers, and being ostracized from their peer group.

Now let us see what happens when distress is projected outward. It leads to aggressive behaviour and temper tantrums. Aggression results due to frustrations and angry feelings. Frequently, children have anger dyscontrol. Anger is a powerful emotion. It tends to erupt when a person perceives a slight, an offence or as being wronged or denied desirable objects, and reacts to the situation by retaliation. It is the psychological interpretation of the situation, to which a reaction is elicited. Anger has been connoted by phrases like 'explode', 'blow your top', 'hit the roof', 'fly off the handle' and 'blow a fuse'. Since anger usually involves reprisal, it can become dangerous to the angered person and to the person who has aroused the anger.

Anger ranges from mild to severe. It has been categorized in seven stages. The first stage, rated as zero, is when one is feeling angry subconsciously but not demonstrating it. A pertinent example is unexplained restlessness in situations that we do not remember, but tend to react negatively every time. The second stage expression of anger is through subtle clues. This can be understood as giving a dirty look and glaring. The third stage is displeasure shown without blaming. This is akin to irritation. The usual examples are recollecting you forgot something after locking the house, forgetting the notebook after completing the homework, etc. The fourth stage indicates anger as a little more displeasure to elicit a response. This is when we express anger by inwardly calling names or shaking our fists.

The fifth stage is when we scowl or use harsh words in combination with clearly visible facial expressions of anger. The sixth stage is when anger is expressed with loud speech and expression of physical threat like shaking one's fist. This is the time when we may be engaged in verbal fighting with expletives and use of harsh and violent words. The last stage is when temper is lost and the person gets into a rage that may lead to aggression. Here a person may be embroiled in actual physical fights that may lead to physical injury or even death. The last two stages are seen in adolescents especially when they indulge in gang activities.

Aggression is angry, hostile behaviour that is intended to hurt or upset others. The emphasis is on the words 'intention' and 'hurt'. In other words, it is a deliberate intention to hurt. Boys are aggressive more often than girls. However, in the normal course of development, nearly every child displays aggressive behaviour to some extent. It is a common phenomenon amongst pre-nursery and nursery school children, that declines during the early school years, becomes prominent again during adolescent years and gradually reduces during adulthood.

Physical aggression can be gauged by behaviours like biting, hitting, shoving, scratching, kicking or snatching objects from other children. *Verbal* aggression is seen in the use of abusive language, bullying, calling names, teasing, blaming and heaping indignities on others. Amongst school children, aggression can be related to *games* (aggression related to the rough and tumble play, predominantly amongst boys), *harassment* (teasing, threatening and physical violence) and *specific hostility* (assertion and aggression related to wanting to achieve certain goals like the teachers' attention).

Truancy is another oft-occurring problem. Truancy is an unexcused absence from school. In other words, the child learns to cut classes either while remaining in school or running away from school. These children characteristically find it difficult to make friends, and have a negative attitude towards school and teachers. The consequence of truancy can be serious as the child may show delinquent behaviour and get in trouble with law enforcing authorities. Later in adult life there is a possibility of developing criminal behaviour.

Bullying is another behavioural disturbance seen amongst persons with LD. Bullying is a form of aggression that encompasses the use of force, threats, intimidation, coercion and abuse. The intent is to hurt another physically, mentally and emotionally. It is never a one-time incidence but repeated and habitual behaviour. It usually occurs when there is an imbalance of social or physical power, i.e., the bully belongs to perceived high social status or has physical superiority. Bullying is also considered as 'acting out behaviour' of depressive feelings.

Such aggressive behaviour is most visible in those who were themselves bullied. In fact, the bullied turned bully is far more vicious, violent and vindictive. Bullying can be both physical and verbal. In physical bullying the victim is kicked, punched and beaten up, bitten, shoved, scratched or manhandled. In verbal bullying the person may be abused, teased, threatened, called names, made the target of sexual or bigoted comments, mimicked and taunted.

These are some of the frequently occurring associated disturbances seen. If at any time you perceive children reacting strangely or differently, be alert to these behavioural changes. Try not to ignore or brush them aside. These disorders can have serious repercussions on the child's mental health and behaviour.

SECTION III

Evaluation and Management of Learning Disabilities

6

Assessment of Learning Disability

Importance and Need for Assessment

As LD IS so varied, with diverse symptoms observed in different children, it was not easy to form a unanimous consensus to its definition. It took countless decades of observations, research and evaluation to understand the concept. Even now there are many aspects and issues that need to be smoothened out for clarity and better cognizance of LD.

The purpose of assessing LD arose after several deliberations. Genuine cases of LD were often confused and clubbed together with children who were inattentive, disruptive or unable to cope with the curriculum, either due to low or borderline intelligence or other conditions. Such children would at some point find themselves out of the school and formal curriculum. So, some kind of screening was required to segregate the truly learning disabled from those who may have other reasons for poor academic performance.

Some other conditions like autism, severe emotional disturbance, behavioural disturbance, ADHD, all have a bearing on the learning process. Neurological conditions like epilepsy and sensory impairment too occur concomitantly with LD. In case one or more of these conditions prevail, LD would become a co-morbid *secondary* condition to any of the above primary disorders, thus compounding the identification process.

Other issues, like lack of language familiarity and/or language impairment of the child, socio-economic status of the parents, parents' education and vocation, all need to be kept in mind before assessment is started. Even environmental conditions of the child—being bred in disadvantaged or marginalized societies, as seen in slum- or ghetto-bred children—would hamper learning. Hence, for the diagnosis of LD one and all factors need to be taken cognizance of before coming to a decision.

Identification of a child with LD is only one aspect of the assessment purpose. A second and equally important facet is the development of a child-specific individualized educational plan (IEP). Once the details of the actual academic performance are documented, it gives an idea of the deficit and strength areas, and a comparison vis-à-vis the peer group and grade-level performance of the child. Therefore, in recent years, criterion-referenced testing, task analysis curriculum-based assessment and responsiveness to instruction have all gathered impetus.[1]

Hence, to assess LD, numerous tests pertinent to academic performance need to be administered. Since LD is not confined to only academic performance but involves non-academic settings too, it is requisite to garner information from all relevant sources. So, information regarding non-academic functioning is also simultaneously gathered from parents, teachers and any reliable informant. Standardized tests are administered by clinical psychologists and special educators who are authorized to certify the disability.

Learning disability, like any other disability, can vary in its severity as mild, moderate and severe. It differs in different age groups from early childhood to adulthood. Hence, the process of assessment would alter according to the age group of the person. Since a child with LD tends to underperform and underachieve academically, many a times children with low intellectual abilities are also termed as having LD. Therefore, before the child is assessed for LD, an intelligence test needs to be administered to rule out intellectual handicap conditions like intellectual disability and borderline intelligence.

To test the child the **criteria of 7+ years of age or being in Class II and above** needs to be strictly followed.

Two Phases of Assessment

Assessment is a two-phase process—in the first phase the clinical psychologist collects information about the child by interviewing the parents and the child. Since the referral largely comes from schools, it is advisable to seek details of the academic performance and the child's behaviour at school, from the teachers. The second phase comprises a Formal Assessment undertaken by a Clinical Psychologist.

Phase I: Clinical Psychologist Collects Information

A 7-year-old boy was referred for testing, on the recommendation of the school. The parents came armed with his notebooks and drawings. They claimed that the school was prejudiced against their son. The notebooks showed that his work was excellently done, with neatness and congratulatory remarks from the teacher. The parents wanted me to give a certificate based on the notebooks alone. However, as is customary, I insisted on meeting the child to which they expressed reluctance as the child would have to miss school to meet me. Nonetheless, I refused to do the needful (provide the certificate) until I had at least met the child and tested him by standardized tests. Later in the day I received a call from the school principal wanting to know my opinion and assessment details. When I told her I could not share these as I had not met the child, she informed me that the child had muscular dystrophy (an inherited disease that damages and weakens the muscles over time) and perhaps had intellectual capabilities less than average. He had severe writing difficulties, poor spellings and comprehension, she added. She wanted the child to be transferred to the special section meant for children with disabilities, where teaching was done at a slower rate in consonance with their condition. However, the parents were not willing to accept this arrangement, as they felt that their child would be deprived of a normal education. In fact, I later came to know that the notebooks shown to me were completed by the elder son. Clearly the parents needed to be counselled.

Though most parents do not resort to such methods, a sizeable group has many fears that predominantly exist in their minds. When one is counselling the parents, sensitivity needs to be maintained to address their fears related to labelling, attached stigma, and compromised future, especially of sons. A gamut of reactions is often seen, right from denial, anger, disbelief to downright rejection of the diagnosis. Their emotional dyscontrol also needs to be dealt with, as parents frequently burden the child with their emotional distress, giving the message to the child that there is no hope for him/her.

Interviewing parents: Before formal assessment is started, some relevant data needs to be collected from parents using the interview technique. The parents are asked questions keeping in mind the following areas to give us specific information about the child.

a) Birth history (in case of any birth trauma);
b) Developmental milestones (at what age he/she started walking, talking and other milestone details);
c) Family history (similar problem in any other family member); and
d) School history (age at which the child went to school, ability to cope with school curriculum, dependency on parents for homework completion and similar details).

Here is a list of probable questions that can be asked to collect information, to indicate whether formal assessment is warranted.

- Did you have any problems/infection during pregnancy?
- Was the delivery normal? Any birth complications?
- Birth weight of the child?
- Whether birth cry was present?
- Were the milestones normal? (Details need to be asked.)
- Any major illness/surgery in infancy or childhood?
- Any history of epileptic seizures, encephalitis or meningitis?
- Has your child complained of eyesight problems?
- Does your child complain of inability to see the blackboard?
- Did you ever get your child's hearing checked/any history of serious ear infection?
- Did the child start school at the right age (4–5 years)?
- Did the child react well to school?

- Does your child complain of dizziness or headaches?
- Is your child right-handed or left-handed?
- Did you try to change the natural 'handedness' of the child? If left-handed did you try to encourage use of right-hand?
- Does your child confuse between right and left?
- Is your child clumsy?
- Does your child fall frequently?
- Does your child find studies very difficult?
- Does the child's attention easily wander?
- Does the child make excuses for not writing?
- Does the child complain of fatigue in hand while writing?
- Is the child's handwriting poor?
- Does the child find it difficult to read and comprehend the text at the same time?
- Does the child learn faster if the text is read to him/her?
- Does the child perform better in oral tests than in written tests?
- Does the child find it difficult to read anything?
- Does the child find it difficult to spell even simple words?
- Does the child find it difficult to express his/her ideas while writing?
- Does the child find it difficult to follow instructions?
- Do you find the child performing well in an applied (practical use of information) than theoretical field?
- Does the child find dealing with numbers difficult?
- Does the child tend to reverse syllables/numbers/alphabets?
- Is your child able to tell the time? (Query only for parents of children older than 8+ years.)

- Has the child remained absent from school for a long time (at least consecutively for 2 weeks or more)?
- Is there any family member from both the parents' families (three generations) who faced similar academic/curriculum difficulties?
- Any other emotional problems the child is experiencing?

Apart from the information collected from the parents, it would be prudent to check the written copies of the child. Samples of written work of English (if first language), second language and mathematics need to be scrutinized to check for signs of LD. One needs to check for reversals, spelling mistakes, grammatical errors and to see if there is a consistent pattern or repetition of same errors.

Inputs from teachers: The request for assessment should rightfully come from the teachers and the school. This unfortunately is not always the case in our country. Ideally both the teachers and the parents should be interviewed. As far as possible while taking the case history, information needs to be gathered from the parents; and, at the very least, a written report must be received from the teachers. Since LD signs may appear from an early age, even in pre-nursery classes, an alert teacher can spot those signs—although, as said in earlier chapters, the early signs are termed as *developmental delay* and not as signs of LD. However, if despite early use of remediation techniques, nil or very little consistent improvement is seen then recommendation needs to be made for formal assessment of LD.

A dialogue between the assessor and teachers needs to be established for collecting relevant information vis-à-vis academic performance, and behaviour in the classroom and in school.

Since teachers are more attuned to the academic expectations from the child, information thus gathered from them has special significance. Also, teachers are better equipped to give information about the kind of mistakes made, repetition of the same errors and whether the performance level is at par with peers and matches the grade level.

Certain queries centred around the academic performance and class behaviour are put to the teachers too. Some probable questions that need to be asked are as follows:

- What has been the academic performance since the beginning of schooling?
- From which class did the academic decline start?
- What is the child's ability to comprehend instructions given in the class?
- What is their ability to follow rules of the class?
- What is their ability to sustain and complete the given task?
- Does the child have difficulty in mastering tasks?
- Does the child have difficulty in translating academic skills (critical/logical thinking) to other tasks requiring these skills and vice versa?
- Does the child need to be guided step by step to complete the task?
- Are many promptings required to complete the task?
- Does the attention of the child waver making it difficult to complete the task?
- Compared to others does the child take longer time to complete the tasks?
- Is the child unable to comprehend the task and so is at a loss to apply problem-solving steps?

- Do the child's grades remain poor despite concerted efforts both by the child and the teacher?
- Does the child have poor memory for both written and spoken information?
- Does the child seem to perform better in oral work, as compared to written?
- Do any significant efforts need to be put in for either expressive or receptive language processing?
- Is there disinterest in studies to the extent that homework and schoolwork appears to be a big burden to the child?
- Are there any signs or symptoms noticeable of any type of LD, especially in languages, mathematics and writing?

Questions related to behaviour in school:

Several years ago, a subdued 12-year-old girl met me with her agitated father. The father informed me that a few days back she had attempted suicide but was not willing to reveal the reason for doing so. As she was his only child, he was frantic with worry. During the interview many interesting school-related issues emerged. Since primary school she had been ostracized in her class as she was shy and exceedingly plain looking and applied oil to her hair. A boy who was the class bully started teasing her as 'teli' (oily). She told her mother about it and asked her not to apply oil to her hair. However, her mother brushed aside these pleas as being nonsensical and disregarded them. Academically too she faltered. Often, she was reprimanded in the class for shoddy work.

As these children grew older, the entire class ganged up with the class bully and she was mercilessly teased by new names like 'cartoon' and 'mug'. Mug is slang for being stupid and also because her hair was plastered with oil, which made her ears stick out prominently. Over the years she was so much isolated in the class that she sat alone, had no one to share her luncheon with, scored disappointingly and had a poor attendance record.

The straw that broke the camel's back, which led to the suicide attempt, was when the class bully and some of his cronies tripped her and as she fell, they pulled her uniform exposing her undergarments. The entire class had laughed uproariously and teased her about the colour of her panties. She dissolved into tears but not a single classmate consoled her. Just prior to this incident, the teacher had scolded her for scoring zilch in mathematics. She had been warned that if her performance did not improve, her notebook would be sent to the principal's office. This meant a summons for the parents to meet the principal and she would certainly be berated at home. She told me that she felt so unwanted, useless and unwelcomed that it was better to end her life than face the daily humiliation. She cried profusely throughout the interview. Surprisingly, she had not told her parents about either the frequent chastisement from the teachers or bullying from the classmates, as she feared that she would not be believed and perhaps be blamed by them for her sorry state. She stated categorically that she did not feel emotionally close to either of her parents and frankly did not trust them.

Psychological tests showed that she had LD and had been struggling with academics as well as bullying in school. She had internalized the problems, suggesting that she had learnt to keep problems within herself.

Since children with LD have behavioural problems, it is appropriate to ask the teachers about the behaviour exhibited in the classroom, on playing fields, in the bus and with the peer group. Since aberrant behaviour, as mentioned in the previous chapter, can be classified as internalizing and externalizing disorders, we can get a glimpse of it by asking some relevant questions.

Internalizing disorders

Internalizing behaviours are those that are inward directed and are seen in cases of anxiety and depression. The children are usually quiet and withdrawn. They are easily upset, highly sensitive, embarrassed when they are the centre of attention and worry more than others about their poor academic performance, especially when discussed publicly. Some queries could elicit information on these behaviours, as one needs to simultaneously treat them while giving help for academic improvement.

- Does the child appear to have poor self-esteem?
- Is the child disorganized?
- Is there reluctance to go to school?
- Appears bored and careless?
- Is withdrawn in school?
- Prefers not to socialize?
- Sits alone in class?
- Appears to have hardly any or no friends?
- Has no one to share the tiffin with?
- Other children seem reluctant to give help to the child?
- Appears anxious and distressed?
- Appears sad, weepy or depressed?
- Complains of stomach-ache or headache or fatigue?
- Often wants to go to the sick room?

Externalizing disorders

The following is a case that displayed the externalizing of a disorder:

A 15-year-old boy was brought to the hospital by his father, who, accidently had read an elaborate plan written with a sketch of a house drawn in his son's notebook. The plan entailed harming a 3-year-old child by throwing acid on her face. It seemed that the little girl's father was the adolescent's physical training (PT) teacher, who had scolded him for coming late. As punishment the PT teacher had made him run round the field three times. At this point the adolescent's father added that his son was certified as being LD and instead of focusing on studies he was becoming wayward and difficult to control. Of late he had started beating his mother for asking him to study.

When the adolescent was interviewed separately, he confided that he had been relentlessly bullied by his classmates and fellow bus passengers for his poor academics and short stature. He was beaten up and called vulgar names for being short and puny since a young age. Henceforth, he had concentrated exclusively on building up his physical strength. Now he was in a position to protect himself but the anger, hatred and, most importantly, the sense of helplessness he had felt then continued to be predominantly present. He actually found pleasure in seeing helplessness in persons whom he bullied. Any perceived insult was assuaged by acts of violence or assault. He categorically said that he had no interest in academics and planned to become a gymnasium trainer.

Externalizing behaviours are directed outwards; such children are often naughty, bossy, loud and cheeky. They tend to be disruptive in class, answer back rudely to the teachers, refuse to cooperate and can even be physically violent. They tend to make fun of and even bully those who are academically superior to them, and treat studies as being frivolous. However, inwardly such children are embarrassed by their failures and feel powerless; hence they try to be brazen about it.

Some questions that could elicit information about such behaviours in the class are as follows:

- Is the child inattentive and restless?
- Is the child disruptive when the teacher is teaching?
- Does the child tend to stare out of the window?
- Does the child prefer to sit at the back of the class?
- Does the child tend to disturb children who are studying?
- Does the child single out and poke fun at studious children?
- Does the child run away with articles belonging to others?
- Does the child act as a bully?
- Is the child verbally and physically aggressive in and outside the class?
- Does the child try to gain attention and acceptability of others by playing the clown?
- Is the child friendlier with under-achievers of the class?
- Does the child purposely blurt out incorrect answers for a laugh?
- Does the child purposely break rules whether in the class, library, bus or during any school-related activities?
- Do the parents complain of unmanageability at home as well?

Children with ADHD would also have some of the behaviours mentioned above. However, ADHD is a neurological condition and may require medical treatment.

Once it is established from the information gathered (from the parents, teachers and scrutinizing the notebooks) that the child is a suitable candidate for testing, then we move towards formal assessment. In case the associated disturbances are present as well then it is advisable to quantify them too.

Phase 2: Conducting a Formal Assessment

A formal assessment encompasses standardized tests to be administered by clinical psychologists, special educators, trained school psychologists and neuropsychologists. In our country a report by these professionals is valid with the two main boards— the Central Board of Secondary Education (CBSE) and the Indian Certificate of Secondary Education (ICSE)—only if these professionals are registered practitioners of the Rehabilitation Council of India (RCI). Other associated professionals like psychometrists, educational specialists, school counsellors, vocational counsellors, speech and language specialists, occupational therapists, physicians and psychiatrists do not conduct LD assessments. However, several states in our country require a psychiatrist to countersign the report.

Assessment entails measuring the psychological processes. This involves various tests. First and foremost, the child is administered an intelligence test. The rationale of starting the testing process with an intelligence test is to rule out intellectual disability, borderline and below average intelligence. An intelligence test gives a composite Intelligence Quotient (IQ) score and two sub-scores—the Verbal Quotient (VQ) score and Performance Quotient (PQ) score. The VQ represents verbal or language-based learning whereas PQ represents visual interpretation, synthesis ability, perception of three-dimensional and two-dimensional figures.

There are innumerable intelligence tests that have been used for assessing the intelligence of children as well as adolescents. Some of the tests routinely used the world over are the Wechsler

Intelligence Scale for Children (WISC), the Stanford-Binet Intelligence Scale and the Kaufman Assessment Battery for Children. Some of these tests have been made culture-friendly in India, with standardized Indian norms. The WISC is known as the Malin's Intelligence Scale for Indian Children (MISIC), and the Stanford-Binet Test with Indian norms is the Binet Kamat Test. Some other commonly used tests for LD are the Woodcock-Johnson Psycho-Educational Battery, the Wide Range Achievement Test and the Kaufman-Johnson Assessment Battery, for children to measure cognitive ability academic skills of reading, writing and mathematics.

Wechsler Intelligence Scale for Children (WISC): The WISC was developed by David Wechsler in 1949 at Bellevue Hospital in New York City. Currently, Wechsler Intelligence Scale for Children-Revised Vth edition (WISC-R V), which was published in 2014, is being used to assess intelligence.[2] It takes about 45–65 minutes to administer and caters to the age range from 6–16 years. The test gives Full Scale IQ and 10 Primary Scale. The various sub-scales are as follows:

a) Similarities Test and Vocabulary Tests that measure verbal comprehension;
b) Block Design Test and Visual Puzzle Test that measure visual spatial ability;
c) Matrix Reasoning and Figure Weights that measure fluid reasoning;
d) Digit Span and Picture Span Tests that measure attention span and working memory; and
e) Coding and Symbol Search that measure processing speed.

Several indices can be established from the WISC-R V test, namely, visual spatial index (VSI), fluid reasoning index (FRI), working memory index (WMI), verbal comprehension index (VCI) and processing speed index (PSI).

The **visual spatial index** measures the non-verbal abilities like rotating and organizing shapes. A poor VSI performance is indicative of mathematical difficulties.

The **fluid reasoning index** indicates the problem-solving ability that is independent of previous exposure or knowledge. It shows the child's ability to apply reasoning in novel situations. A low FRI performance is indicative of deficit in inductive reasoning and poor generalization from previous experience.

The **working memory index** checks the child's ability for attention sustenance. It predicts the attention span and recent memory of the child. A poor WMI score would suggest presence of Attention Deficit Disorder or ADD. Presence of good short-term memory is relevant for grasping and retaining of read material.

The WISC-R V **verbal comprehension index** measures reasoning ability, language development, understanding concepts and general knowledge. Poor VCI scores strongly suggest difficulty in reading and academics.

The **processing speed index** measures the speed of performing perceptual-motor activities. PSI measures a child's ability to scan and understand visual information. Poor PSI would hamper the speed of reading comprehension, writing and mathematics.

Thus, apart from the test being used as an exclusion test to separate normal children from those who are below average and intellectually deficient, the various indices help the clinician to gain insight into the key assets and capabilities that can be used for remediation purposes.

The Indian version of this test with Indian norms was developed by Dr Arthur J. Malin in 1969.[3] Since the original WISC appeared culturally unfair for the Indian children, as test items were pertinent to Western culture, a lot of items were replaced. It was made more culture-friendly for Indian children, and hence was renamed as **Malin's Intelligence Scale for Indian Children** or, in short, as **MISIC**. It can be administered to school-going children ranging between the ages of 6–15 years and 11 months. It takes roughly 60–90 minutes to administer it.

There are eleven subtests, of which six represent the verbal scale and five the performance scale. Verbal tests include the following subtests—Information, Comprehension, Arithmetic, Similarity, Vocabulary and Digit Span. The performance tests are Picture Completion, Block Design, Object Assembly, Coding and Mazes.

It is a point-scale test. The raw scores are converted into standardized Test Quotients (TQ) per age level ranging from 6 to 15 years. The TQs are summated, and their mean score calculated to give three indices namely Intelligence Quotient (IQ), Verbal Quotient (VQ) and Performance Quotient (PQ). In other words, the six verbal subtests are summed up and divided by 6 to give the Verbal Quotient; similarly the five performance subtests are added and divided by 5 to give the Performance Quotient. The average of VQ and PQ gives the IQ score.

The table needs to be so indicated:

Subtest	TQ	Category
Information	83	Below Average
Comprehension	111	Above Average
Arithmetic	80	Below Average

Subtest	TQ	Category
Similarities	98	Average
Vocabulary	102	Average
Digit Span	90	Average
Picture Completion	82	Below Average
Block Design	112	Above Average
Object Assembly	95	Average
Coding	105	Average
Mazes	130	Very Superior

Figure 9: Specimen of scores on MISIC

Stanford-Binet Test: The Simon-Binet scale to measure intelligence was created by the French psychologist Alfred Binet and his student Theodore Simon in 1905. Lewis M. Terman of Stanford University in 1911 revised it for the American population and renamed it as Stanford-Binet Test. Currently, its Vth edition (SB5) under Roid's direction was published in 2003, and is still being used.[4] It caters to the age range of 2–85+ years. This test is popularly used for diagnostic purposes for developmental and intellectual deficiencies, early childhood assessment, tracking the development of the growing brain, psycho-educational evaluations for special education services especially for slow learners, career development and planning, neurological deficits, and giftedness.[5]

The test measures cognitive and intellectual abilities. It has both verbal and performance items numbering 52. The test measures five weighted factors—knowledge, visual-spatial processing, fluid reasoning, quantitative reasoning and working memory. Each weighted factor tends to compute different abilities:

- **Knowledge** is comprised of vocabulary, procedural knowledge (non-verbal) and picture absurdities (non-verbal);

- **Visual-spatial** subtests include form board and form patterns (non-verbal), and position and direction;

- **Fluid reasoning** consists of early reasoning, verbal absurdities, verbal analogies and object series matrices (non-verbal);

- **Quantitative reasoning** includes non-verbal quantitative reasoning and verbal quantitative reasoning; and

- **Working memory** contains delayed response (non-verbal), block span (non-verbal), memory for sentences and last word.

The reliability and validity of the test is well established.

Binet Kamat Test (BKT): The Indian version of the Stanford Binet Test is known as the Binet Kamat Test as it was adapted by Dr V.V. Kamat in 1967.[6] There has been no subsequent revision of the test. It is an age scale ranging from age 3 to superior adult level, which is 22 years. Each age range has six items with every item being scored as two months. For example, five correct responses would mean a score of 10 months. The correct responses are summated to represent the score of that year. The test items are consecutively for 3 to 10 years of age, and thereafter for alternative years. Hence, there are no items or alternative items for ages 11, 13, 15, 17, 18, 20, 21 years. From age 11 to 17 years, each test item represents four months and for ages 18 to 22 each test item constitutes six months. Apart from the usual six items, alternative items are also given for each age level measured by the test.

The BKT gives us an Intelligence Quotient (IQ) score, Basal Age (where the child has answered all the items correctly) and Terminal Age (where the child has not answered any item correctly). The obtained IQ needs to be prorated to make it comparable to World Health Organization (WHO) IQ ranges. Pattern analysis can be done to give age level for abilities measured. The BKT assesses the following areas: language, meaningful memory, non-meaningful memory, conceptual thinking, non-verbal reasoning, numerical reasoning, visuo-motor skills and social intelligence. Currently, the BKT is the most useful test in our country to assess children and adults with intellectual disability and in some cases, slow learners.

Intelligence tests are used as exclusion criterion too. In other words, if the IQ is less than 85 and above 79 the child is termed as a slow learner. If the IQ is less than 70, the child falls in the intellectual deficiency category. Such children are not tested further for LD. Those children who have an IQ of 85 that is in the average or any category above, are subjected to further testing by administering the LD battery.

Learning disability batteries: Several LD batteries have been used over the decades. Here, only a few that are in current use in our country, are described below:

Wide Range Achievement Test (WRAT): The Wide Range Achievement Test (WRAT) is, as the name suggests, an achievement test.[7] It measures a child's ability to read, spell, comprehend and compute. The test was developed by Sidney W. Bijou and Joseph Jastak in 1941. However, there have been several editions and currently it is in its fifth edition, revised by Gary S. Wilkinson and Gary J. Robertson. The test can be administered to an extensively large age range, from 5–94 years. The test has two equivalent forms named as Blue and Green. The advantage of two forms is that retesting is possible within a short span of time, without the fear of seeing the practice effect of previous exposure. If need be, the two forms can also be administered together on the same person.

The Wide Range Achievement Test, Fifth Edition-India (**WRAT5-India**), is so called as it is available in English as well as in many Indian languages like Hindi, Marathi, Kannada and Tamil.[8] It is easy to administer and this test is a precise measure to assess the reading, spelling and mathematical skills in children from the age range of 6 years to 19 years and 11 months. It is frequently used by clinical psychologists to diagnose LD.

The advantages of this version of the test are: (i) that it can be administered to individuals as well as in small groups (though not all subtests); (ii) only those subtests need be administered that are required. The entire battery is not a prerequisite for dispensation of results and diagnosis.

Traditionally it is a paper–pencil test, but the digital version is also available, where scoring and report are digitally obtainable. This cuts administration time to as little as 10 minutes for younger children, and approximately 30–45 minutes for the older children and young adults. The scoring rules are explicit, reducing ambiguity and enhancing the accuracy of the test findings. Hence, the test can be scored in three ways—manually; Q-global; and Q-interactive. Naturally the identification of the LD is precise, thereby reducing the false positive cases.

The test measures the skills related to reading, sentence comprehension, spellings and mathematical computation.

The Word Reading test measures the ability to recognize alphabet and words. The words are arranged in increasing difficulty level. The test begins with easy words and graduates to difficult words. It is not a timed test. The child has to read aloud, and the administrator keeps a track of mispronunciation, reversals of phonemes, inability to read a word, hesitation in reading the word, and fluency. Fluency here refers to whether the word was read with all the phonemes intact, or whether the child needed to break the word into individual phonemes to be able to read it out.

Sentence Comprehension test measures the ability to read, comprehend and complete the sentence by filling in a word or a series of words using the cloze technique. In cloze technique words are systematically removed from the text and the child has to fill the appropriate word keeping the context of the sentence in mind. The child either reads it aloud or silently. Again, this subtest is arranged in order of difficulty, starting with very easy items. In all there are 50 items. It also gives an understanding about the vocabulary attainment of the child. This is an untimed subtest.

Together, the scores on Word Reading and Sentence Comprehension tests give a Composite Score that displays the reading ability of the child.

Some guidelines that reflect the common mistakes seen in reading are as follows:

a) Reverses letters, words or numbers—'b' is reversed for 'd', 'p' for 'q', 'm' for 'w', and 'was' for 'saw'. Will read 'bog' for 'dog', 'gril' for 'girl', 'ded' for 'bed', and 'P' for '9';

b) Ignores punctuations like full stop and comma—will stop at any place in the text, or continue to read even when there is a full stop;

c) Substitutes similar looking words, which may not have any connection with the text—'helmet' for 'hamlet', 'horse' for 'house', 'sunrise' for 'surprise';

d) Substitutes dissimilar words also, although the general meaning may be the same—'laugh' for 'giggle', 'cry' for 'weep';

e) Functional words like 'a', 'an', 'the', 'were', 'to' may usually be missing;

f) Suffixes and prefixes are quite often missing—'want' for 'want*ed*', and 'understand' for 'understand*ing*'; and 'lame' as 'blame' and 'exterior' as 'texterior'.

g) Reading is so slow and with so much effort that the text is either not understood at all, or only partially understood.

The Spelling test measures the child's ability to write letters and words when given dictation. There is no time limit. This subtest measures three distinct entities of writing, namely ability to spell, to form letters and to form words. Here are some guidelines to help understand what needs to be gleaned from this subtest.

To check for spelling errors:

a) Spelling errors are similar to reading errors;

b) Even simple words are misspelt—'thy' for 'they', 'hte' for 'the', 'wen' for 'when';

c) Reversals are seen in alphabets—'b' as 'd', 'q' as 'p';

d) Reversals of phonemes (word sounds) in words as 'kitchen' being written as **'kict/in'**, 'equipment' as **'i/qu/ment'**, 'correction' as 'chgction'. The phonemes are jumbled for correction and the 'p' phonetic is missing in spelling of equipment.

e) Mirror imaging may be present mostly in the use of letters 'c', 's', 'e' and 't'.

f) Marked use of erasers, crossing out words and overwriting.

Guidelines to check for writing errors:

a) It is usually messy and poorly integrated;

b) Pencils are gripped tightly so that the fingers get cramped;

c) The rule of writing capital and small letters is ignored—capital letters may be in the middle of the sentence, or the sentence may begin with a small letter;

d) The letters may not sit properly on the line;

e) Words may either be widely spaced or crushed closely together, running into each other;

f) Margins are seldom used;

g) Writing anything takes a long time; and

h) Cursive writing is difficult to master especially capital letters. Confusion is seen in alphabets like 'f' and 'b', 'w' and 'u', and 'm' and 'n'.

The Mathematical Computation test is timed and measures the ability to identify numbers, calculate, count and solve simple oral mathematical problems using the operations of addition and subtraction. Written mathematics involves complex operations like multiplication, division, decimals, simple algebra, geometry and advanced fractions.

Guidelines to check for type of errors:

a) Reversal in numbers as 41 read as 14, 17 as 71;

b) Difficulty in gauging 'bigger than' and 'less than' phenomena;

c) Has difficulty in doing sums that involve the multiplication table; and

d) Has difficulty in remembering scientific facts that involve numbers, like, pi (π) is 3.14.

Scoring and results of the subtests: The raw score of each subtest is tabulated, which includes oral as well as written scores. The raw scores are converted into Standard scores, with reference to age of the child. This is evaluated against three Confidence Levels—85 per cent, 90 per cent and 95 per cent. The test gives the Percentile ranks and Optional scores that includes Grade Equivalent, Normal Curve Equivalent (NCE) and Stanine scores. The obtained scores can also be compared as the performance on each subtest can be weighed against each other. This gives an idea as to which area needs more attention for remediation.

NIMHANS Index for Specific Learning Disabilities: Hirisave et al., from NIMHANS, developed a test in 1991, assessing SLDs.[9] The test consists of various subtests to measure skills related to reading, writing, spelling and computation. It consists of two levels.

Level I: This is a pre-academic assessment for children between the ages of 5–7 years. It includes tests on: Attention, Visual Discrimination, Visual Memory, Auditory Memory, Speech and Language, Visuo-motor Skills and Writing Skills.

Level II: This focuses on the academic performance of children from Classes I–VII and consists of tests on: Attention; Language (that includes reading, writing, comprehension and spelling); Perceptual Motor Abilities; Memory; and Arithmetic.

The various tests that are part of the NIMHANS SLD battery are:[10]

i. Attention test (quick cancellation of specific numbers from a given list);

   ii. Visuo-motor skills (the Bender Gestalt test and the Developmental test of Visuo-Motor integration);

  iii. Auditory and Visual Processing (discrimination and memory);

  iv. Reading, writing, spelling and comprehension;

   v. Speech and Language, including Auditory behaviour (Receptive Language) and Verbal expression; and

  vi. Arithmetic (Addition, subtraction, multiplication, division and fraction)

The importance of the NIMHANS SLD battery is that it has been developed in India, its trials have been conducted on Indian population, and has Indian norms. It has kept in mind the education system and the languages used in the country. Recently, the Government of India and various Indian courts have decreed that NIMHANS Index for Specific Learning Disabilities is a reliable and valid test for assessing disability.

Some Recommended Tests:

The Woodcock-Johnson Psycho-Educational Battery: This was developed by Richard W. Woodcock, a U.S. psychologist, and his business partner Mary E. Bonner, in 1977.[11] This test is in its third revision. It is a comprehensive test that evaluates everyone from preschool children to the geriatric population.

The test is divided into two parts. Part I consists of twelve subtests that cater to academic ability and aptitude. Part II has ten subtests and is exclusively for measuring academic achievement. Interestingly, the norms are proportioned to match the exact distribution of sex-by-race, region-by-urbanization, and occupational status of the U.S. population. The tests of cognitive ability produce a full-scale intelligence score that indicates both the strength and weakness of the candidate's information processing. The subtests that monitor the academic achievement provide information about the level of reading, written language, mathematics and basic knowledge skills.

The test is widely used as a diagnostic tool for identifying SLD. The advantage of this test is that when the finding of the cognitive portion is combined with the achievement portion it discloses the learning style of the child. It also gives the discrepancy between the potential and actual performance.

The Kaufman Assessment Battery for Children (KABC): The KABC was developed by Alan S. Kaufman and Nadeen L. Kaufman in 1983 and later revised in 2004.[12] The test has been translated into many different languages, as it is a diagnostic clinical instrument used for assessing cognitive development. The advantage of this test is that it assesses handicapped groups and the learning disabled. Being culture-free, it is helpful for linguistic minorities too.

However, KABC needs to be complemented with intelligence tests like the Wechsler Adult Intelligence Scale, or its child version the Wechsler Intelligence Scale for Children, the Stanford-Binet Test, or neuropsychological tests.

Writing the Report

A report should be descriptive and detailed. It should carry the child's name, age, class and school details, reason for assessment, date on which the test is conducted and name of the tests administered. A brief history of the child would be helpful in recording any other disorders that may be present.

Given below is a sample report of the test findings of a male student in Class VII:

A Sample Report

Test Findings:

On MISIC his IQ is 95 that falls in the average category. His Verbal Quotient (VQ) is 90 and Performance Quotient (PQ) is 99. Pattern analysis shows the following:

Subtest	TQ	Category
Information	96	Average
Comprehension	94	Average
Arithmetic	81	Below Average
Similarities	104	Average
Vocabulary	94	Average
Digit Span	72	Borderline
Picture Completion	106	Average
Block Design	92	Average
Object Assembly	75	Borderline
Coding	93	Average
Mazes	130	Very Superior

Digit Span indicates poor attention span. Object Assembly test indicates poor synthesis ability.

Dyslexia Battery, WRAT, shows the following:

Subtest/Composite	Raw Score	Standard Score	Confidence Interval 95%	Optional Score/ Grade Equivalent
Word Reading	41	87	79-86	4.2

Subtest/Composite	Raw Score	Standard Score	Confidence Interval 95%	Optional Score/ Grade Equivalent
Sentence Comprehension	9	67	60-76	1.7
Spelling	26	84	76-94	3.9
Mathematics Computation	33	88	80-97	5.1
Reading Composite	154	75	79-92	_________

Reading skills—English: On the Word Reading test his performance is of Grade 4.2. Paragraph reading shows that fluency is fair. Despite fair fluency, the comprehension of the read text—especially difficult sentences—is lost by the time he finishes reading the sentence. He sometimes breaks the word into phonemes to try reading it. Reversals in phonemes is more often present. He often tends to guess words and reads by approximation. He needs to work hard in improving his reading skills.

Hindi: Reading skills in Hindi is average. His fluency is fair. He tends to guess words and reads by approximation. He still does not recognize all Hindi alphabets. Confusion is seen in similar sounding alphabets. He needs to work on matras and sanyukthakshar. Like in English, he tends to break words into phonemes to read, though not very often. He tends to skip words while reading. He needs to work hard on his reading skills.

English Comprehension: On this subtest his performance is of Grade 1.7. He was able to only complete the easy items. The reading is somewhat laboured, especially when the difficulty level was higher. Hence, by the time he finishes reading the sentence the meaning is lost. ***The sentences were neither read out to him nor translated in Hindi.*** He needs to work very hard. His vocabulary needs improvement for finding appropriate words to complete the sentences. There were innumerable spelling mistakes. His writing is sometimes untidy and fairly illegible, especially where he is guessing the answer.

Writing (Copying) skills—English: Copying skills are fair. His writing is untidy and fairly illegible. At times he forgets the concept of capital and small letter. He tends to make many spelling mistakes. He often misses words while copying. The rules of writing are still not learnt.

Writing (Copying) skills—Hindi: Copying skills are fair. His writing is fairly illegible and untidy. He tends to make many spelling mistakes. He often misses words while copying. Some similar sounding alphabets were interchanged while writing.

Spelling skills—English: On Spelling Test his Grade level is 3.9. He has still not learnt the phonetic sounds of the vowels and arbitrarily writes the known word instead of listening to the word dictated. For example, 'material' was written as 'mutirel', 'exaggerate' as 'xgagative', 'excuse' as 'secuse' and so on. Reversals in phonemes are seen. He is not able to pick basic phoneme sounds to spell the words.

Hindi: In word dictation of Class VII, he has got 5 spellings correct out of 15. He has difficulty in putting matras and sanyuktashar. In many places he has put the alphabet instead of the matras. He has difficulty in picking up phonemes, i.e., basic sounds of the word. Problems are specially seen in similar sounding alphabets. He requires to put in more hard work.

Mathematical ability: He has got a Grade level of 5.1. He has scored well in oral mathematics and able to do some complex written sums too. He has average grasp of concepts taught to him. He has understood the basic principles of addition, multiplication, subtraction, division, long multiplication, carry over addition, fractions, and greater than and less than concepts. There are no reversals.

WRAT is indicating learning disabilities of dyslexia (reading) and dysorthographia (spelling).

Summary:

On MISIC his IQ is 95 that falls in the average category. His Verbal Quotient (VQ) is 90 and Performance Quotient (PQ) is 99. **WRAT is indicating learning disabilities of dyslexia (reading) and dysorthographia (spelling).**

Recommendations:

- Teaching him by visual aids would help him to pick the concepts.
- Remediation teaching for spellings would be helpful.
- Extra writing of one page of both English and Hindi would be helpful.
- Rewriting the wrong spellings would benefit him as overlearning of the spellings would be retained in memory.
- Frequent revision of phonetics would benefit him.
- Extra reading would help him.
- It would be encouraging if he is judged more for oral work than written work.

- He will benefit if the school supports him in terms of extra time, not deducting marks for spellings.
- He would benefit if a reader and scribe is provided to him during examinations.
- He needs lots of encouragement to increase his self-esteem.
- Contingency Reinforcement will keep his motivation high.
- Any other skills or hobbies can be encouraged to enhance feeling of self-worth.
- Parents need to be counselled to tone down expectations.

The report should close with recommendations for further guidance for teachers and parents. When tested positive for multiple disorders, the report should recommend exemptions and accommodations given as per the guidelines of the Board (CBSE) or the Council (ISCE).

Assessing Emotional/Associated Disturbances

As we already know, LD causes many emotional and associated disturbances. There are innumerable tests to measure emotional disturbances in children. Only some of the tests that are frequently used by clinicians are described here.

Objective Tests

Self-esteem: This is one of the most compromised feeling states for any person with LD. To measure self-esteem, the Culture-free Self-Esteem Inventory developed by James Battle is frequently used.[13] It has three versions catering to different age groups. The Primary form is meant for children of ages 6–8 years and has 29 items of the dichotomous 'yes' and 'no' variety. It takes less than 15 minutes to administer and measures Global Self-esteem. The second Primary form is meant for older children from 9–12 years of age. This test contain 64 items, of the 'yes-no' type as above. This test measures Academic Self-Esteem, General Self-Esteem, Parental/Home Self-Esteem and Social Self-Esteem.

The third is the Adolescent form, meant for 13–18-year-olds and has 67 items, again of the 'yes-no' kind. This form measures Academic Self-Esteem, General Self-Esteem, Parental/Home Self-Esteem, Social Self-Esteem and Personal Self-Esteem subscales. All the three different forms give a Global Self-Esteem Quotient and Defensiveness scores.

Depression: The Children's Depression Inventory (CDI) was developed by Maria Kovacs in 1979, and was revised as CDI2 in 2011.[14] It is a 27-item test that takes 5–10 minutes to complete. It is a self-rated, symptom-oriented tool to measure depression and dysthymia (low mood that has persisted for more than two years) in children and young adolescents. It measures five aspects of the mood states—negative mood represented by irritability or anger; negative self-esteem; interpersonal problems; anhedonia (inability to enjoy previously enjoyable activities); and ineffectiveness.[15]

Anxiety: Anxiety is another condition strongly associated with LD. Two scales are commonly used for assessment. The State-Trait Anxiety Inventory for Children (STAIC) and Screen for Childhood Anxiety Related Emotional Disorder (SCARED).[16, 17]

Spielberger et al. developed STAIC in 1973.[18] The test is based on his own theory that there is a difference between a general proneness to anxiety that is rooted in one's personality, versus experiencing momentary or fleeting anxiety in an emotional state. The STAIC S-Anxiety consists of 20 statements on a 4-point rating scale that asks the respondent's emotional reaction to a particular situation. These statements can be read to children whose reading ability may yet not be well-developed. The test also contains another 20 statements that cater to how the respondent generally feels. The scores range from 20–80. The test caters to ages from 5–16 years, i.e., from upper elementary to junior high-school children.

SCARED, as mentioned above, was developed by Boris Birmaher et al. in 1999. It is a screening tool to identify anxiety disorders, that includes panic attacks, school phobia, social phobia, separation anxiety, generalized anxiety and also gives an overall score of anxiety. It has 41 items based on a 3-point rating scale ranging from 'not at all true' to 'very true'. It is meant for the ages 8–18 years. The advantage of this test is that it also has a parent version. Together, both the self-assessed child version and the parental version, give a composite anxiety score.

Projective Tests

Often with children it is difficult to elicit information, especially when they are emotionally disturbed. Since children do not articulate well, and may not have high verbal skills, projective tests are used for extracting covert (hidden) and conflict-related information. Projective tests are so designed that the person responds to ambiguous stimuli, and projects own thoughts and emotions to situations or persons. Some of those tests that are useful with children will be described here.

Children's Apperception Test (CAT): The Children's Apperception Test by Bellak and Bellak was developed for children between the ages 3–10 years.[19] There are 10 cards with black and white drawings showing anthropomorphized animals (attributing human characteristics or behaviour to animals). The basic assumption of using animals is that certain animals are less threatening than humans for young children. Children who are very young are encouraged to relate the story and this is written verbatim by the administrator of the test. Children who are a little older and have developed writing skills, write it themselves. The intention behind this test is to elicit information about the growing personality, emotional maturity and psychological health of the child.

A parallel version—called the Children's Apperception Test-Human (CAT-H) using human figures—is also available for older children.[20, 21]

Draw a Person Test (DAPT): The 'Draw a Person Test' was initially the brainchild of Goodenough in 1926 and was then devised by Karen Machover in 1948.[22,23] It was initially a substitute for intelligence tests but it was later found to bring forth creditable and normally unattainable information from young children when they were distressed.

The child is asked to draw a person of either gender—this is not specified by the test administrator—and both direct and indirect questions are asked while the child is still drawing. Questions could pertain to family, interpersonal relationships, school, and certain distressing incidents and so on. The test takes about 10–15 minutes: the figure drawing takes 5 minutes. The test reveals the child's emotional distress, depression, traumas, family relationships, physical and emotional abuse, and anxieties.

Sentence Completion Test (SCT): In 1950, Julian B. Rotter and Janet E. Rafferty devised a test that came to be known as Rotter Incomplete Sentence Blank.[24] It has three forms for different age groups. There are 40 incomplete sentences that the person has to complete with the first thought that comes to their mind. The test caters to the person's relationship with family that includes father, mother, siblings and attitude towards family, school, self-concept, future, peer group, interpersonal relationships and conflictual relationships.

Rorschach Inkblot Test: This is another projective test, but is seldom used with young children.[25] However, this test can extract useful data from adolescents. It consists of 10 cards with totally ambiguous inkblots, to which the person's perceptions are recorded. The responses provide information about the person's thoughts, emotions, needs, motives, conflicts, inner tensions, and personal and interpersonal perceptions.

A 14-year-old girl, who had been labelled as LD when she was 8 years old, was brought to the hospital directly from her school. She had blanked out during her examinations and could not write even a single word in her examination copy. While interviewing her she said that despite reading so well for this particular subject when she saw the question paper, she could not recall anything. She felt so anxious that she had a panic attack and felt faint. Since she was still exceedingly anxious, she was helped to relax with Jacobson's Progressive Muscular Relaxation technique. She was asked to come again the next day for assessments.

A battery of tests were administered, namely Personality Test, projective tests like Sentence Completion Test, Children's Apperception Test (H), Self-esteem Test and Depression and Anxiety tests. The tests indicated that she had a very low self-esteem, mild depression and very high anxiety. The CAT (H) stories indicated that she had gradually lost her friends because of poor academic performance, felt isolated and rejected in her class. She had an extremely poor self-concept and constantly called herself 'loser'. Though she was learning classical vocal and had been performing on stage both in school and musical festivals, she still felt she was 'good-for-nothing'.

In the time she took to complete a chapter, her classmates would finish half the course. She was so discouraged that she had refused to make future plans. Of late even music was not giving her solace. The tests clearly indicated that her thoughts were negative about herself and her confidence was at its lowest ebb. She was taken up for psychotherapy, as her remediation classes were already well organized.

Differential Diagnosis

The testing work of the clinical psychologist does not end with the tests described above. There are many conditions, as mentioned in earlier chapters, that may be confused or run co-currently with LD. Hence, they need to be identified if they co-exist with the primary condition of LD, thereby necessitating the formulation of differential diagnoses. Differential diagnosis refers to either a disorder, or a set of symptoms that need to be differentiated, as they closely resemble the clinical features of the disorder under study.

Several conditions that may comorbidly exist with LD are as follows:

a) Intellectual disability, in which every domain of development is delayed or retarded.

b) Pervasive Development Disorder is when delays are seen in two or more developmental domains. Since it is pervasive, the deficits are visible throughout life.

c) Autism is a pervasive development disorder where impairment is seen in communication, language, and social and emotional functioning. Intelligence differs in autistic children from high-functioning intelligence to intellectual disability.

d) Primary sensory deficits that include vision, hearing, motor and speech; deficits in any of the senses mentioned above nullify the diagnosis of LD, as each of these senses are imperative for learning.

e) Primary Language deficit indicates that language is underdeveloped whereas the non-verbal development is normal.

f) Environmental factors can also comorbidly exist with LD, such as deprivation, insufficient instruction in learning due to poor or inadequate education of parents, and physical or emotional abuse.

g) Identifying slow learners whose IQ is below 85 but above 70. Below 70 which is deemed as intellectual disability which was earlier referred to as mental defective.

Team: A team of professionals is required to help in assessing the above-mentioned functions. These include many branches that are required to work as an interdisciplinary team. Though each professional's inputs are not required for every child, but a fair number of them do get included.

Deficits in the two senses of hearing and vision require the services of an *Audiologist* and *Ophthalmologist* respectively.

A *speech therapist* checks for speech development and deficits.

A *neurologist* is required for brain-related deficits, as seen in: motor movements of gait (walk); unusual movements, a hand-grip that includes an extraordinarily strong grip on the pencil, or easy fatiguability in the hand while writing; soft neurological signs like impaired fine motor skills, abnormal motor tone or abnormal involuntary movements, and any history of seizures.

An *occupational therapist* is required for assessing and treating impaired motor movements. They also try to correct the visual motor coordination that is essential for handwriting.

A *child psychiatrist* may be required to prescribe medication for certain conditions like ADHD and autism; emotional disturbances like depression and anxiety; and behavioural issues like aggression and anger.

A *paediatrician* to see to the overall well-being of the child. This includes keeping a record of the developmental milestones, general health, deficiencies of iron and calcium, imbalances in thyroid or any other hormone.

The *clinical psychologist* needs access to the reports of all the above experts, and the findings of the abovementioned IQ and SLD battery tests, to come to any final conclusion regarding an LD diagnosis.

7
Management of Learning Disability

ONCE THE ASSESSMENT is complete and we are certain that the child has LD and/or any associated problems, we are then able to formulate a plan of action to help the child. This requires a careful analysis of assessments done to link the findings of each test. Relevant information is extracted from every test to discern the degree of severity of the disability, construct the learning profile of the child and make recommendations for an individualized educational plan.

The Individualized Education Plan (IEP), as the very name suggests, is formed to meet the individual educational needs of a child with LD. The programme thus formed keeps in mind both the deficit areas and assets indicated by the psychological test results. The objectives of the plan are threefold. Firstly, to identify long-term goals; secondly, to make meaningful and achievable goals; and thirdly, to have short-term goals for giving instructions that can be observed and assessed. This plan is to assist teachers, special educators, parents and any other personnel involved. The child is also taken into confidence to get full cooperation.

Preparing the Child and Place of Study

The clinical psychologist, or the special educator, needs to prepare the child before any remediation teaching is done. Rapport with the child needs to be established. The purpose of the remediation teaching is conveyed in a reassuring manner, and care is taken to convey it rather as an addition to existing curriculum than as punishment or debasement.

The study space should be clean, uncluttered, airy and well lit. As far as possible the room should have a pleasant feel. The parents need to ensure dedicated study hours. The vicinity of the study room should be quiet. Adequate breaks should be given, and firm resumption of studies also needs to take place. It would be beneficial if the entire family cooperated during the study hours, to not interrupt or create noise. The parent or special educator, too, needs to be attentive and not be distracted by mobile phones or similar gadgets. If the teacher is distracted so would the child be.

Two simple strategies are helpful. If the child is easily distracted, then ask the child to read aloud. Hearing one's own voice helps to bring back the focus. It is beneficial to alternate difficult and easy subjects. This strategy is more effective with older children. Each subject should be earmarked with small portions so that the allotted amount is over the same day. This gives the child a sense of accomplishment plus there is no pending work for the next day. Perception of increased burden is never taken well by children, with or without LD.

Remediation

There are no known medications or other medical procedures that can cure LD. However, these children can be helped by certain scientific techniques to improve their skills. Remediation teaching is carried out for reading, writing, spellings and mathematics. Some exercises can be built to enhance the attention span. Play methods have also been devised that can help in reinforcing the directionality, i.e., distinguishing between right and left. Though these methods are not yet empirically validated, they have shown to be effective in daily practice.

Reading

The basic problem amongst the learning disabled, especially amongst dyslexic children, is their difficulty in processing language. In reading disability, the stumbling block is the understanding of the concept of phonics and breaking them into phonemes.

Phonemic awareness is the understanding that our speech is made up of certain series of sounds that we manipulate while speaking. These sounds are converted into words that we understand, relate to and communicate with. This process involves the ability to *hear* individual sounds and *manipulate* sounds in words.

Phonics refers to the *seeing and using letter sounds* and other rules to sound words. It is both a visual and an oral skill. **Phonemes**, on the other hand, are not visual letter symbols but *sound symbols*. Phonemes are considered one of the best predictors of reading skills. Children who lack awareness of phonemes do not profit by instructions only in phonics, but need to be trained in phonemes as well to develop reading skills.

It is best to give them a rationale by explaining that each word is made up of certain sounds and these sounds are written in a certain order so that the words carry a meaning that makes sense. Therefore, it is important to learn the alphabetic-phonic system.

To begin teaching phonemes it is important to first familiarize the child with the phonetic sound of letters. Begin with the consonants that have a *single* sound, like:

- b, d, f, h, j, k, l, m, n, p, q, r, t, v, x and z.

Once the consonants are mastered, teach the vowels:

- a, e, i, o, u.

The sound that 'y' makes is also somewhat like the sound of a vowel, so it can be taught next.

Simple Word Families can be utilized to understand the vowels.

bat	bet	bit	cot	but
cat	get	fit	dot	cut
fat	let	kit	got	hut
hat	met	lit	hot	nut
mat	pet	pit	jot	put

Figure 10: Sample of Simple Word Families

Then teach the common consonant digraphs. These emerge when two consonants together produce a new sound, like:

- ch, sh, th, wh, pr, pl, ph, bh, and so on.

Once the sound has been mastered, then comes relating the sound with the alphabet. Word families can be used for this purpose.

oo	book, cook, look, hook
ai	Gain, rain, main, pain
ay	way, may, pay, lay
aw	saw, paw, law, raw
ea	head, read, bead, bread
ie	chief, thief, grief, belief
oa	boat, coat, moat, float
ow	cow, bow, mow, sow
pr	prow, pray, prose, prey
ph	phase, phone, photo, physician
pl	Plant, please, plot, play
sh	Share, shot, sharp, shoot
ch	Chair, choir, chip, chop
th	Thin, thick, threw, thought
ou	Mouth, pout, cloud, dough

Figure 11: Sample of Digraph Word Family

In the normal teaching method, we align the letter with the word, for the child to remember, e.g., 'a is for apple', 'b is for ball'. But here the teaching is reversed. Since the child is already familiar with the spoken language and knows the usage of words, aligning the word with the alphabet makes it easier for them to remember. So

Apple begins with a

Ball begins with b

Cat begins with c
and so on.

Phonetics is taught in pre-primary, so one can face resistance from the child. Play methods can easily reinforce the learning.

A big chart showing the alphabet, the corresponding phonetic sound and a picture of the word starting from that alphabet, can be pasted alongside. For example, the alphabet 'a', its corresponding phonetic sound 'ae', and the picture of 'apple' or 'aeroplane' would indicate the association. The chart should carry all the alphabets from A–Z. Such a chart can be put up in the study room and in any other room where the child spends maximum time—to take advantage of both incidental and accidental learning.

Other methods to revise phonetics could include use of flash cards. You can keep a box and mix the flash cards of all the alphabets. Pick any alphabet, e.g., 'D', and ask the child to tell you the associated phonetic sound attached to it. Similarly, you can fill a box with pictures cut from old newspapers or magazines, and ask the child to identify the first phonetic sound that the picture represents. For example, pick up the picture of a dog and ask the child what alphabet the word 'dog' begins with, or what alphabet the word 'cow' begins with. Other games that can help are 'Queen of Sheba' or word games.

The PASS Reading Enhancement Programme is considered effective in enhancing reading skills. It is based on the PASS theory of intelligence.[1,2] There are 10 tasks to which the child is exposed. Since reading skills involve 'cognitive', 'mastering' and 'automaticity', these tasks are built to improve them. Thereby, 4 tasks focus on successive processing enhancement, 4 on simultaneous processing enhancement, and 2 concentrate on developing both successive and simultaneous processing abilities. The 10 tasks are: Joining Shapes, Connecting Letters, Window Sequencing, Transportation Matrices, Related Memory Set, Tracking, Shape Design, Shapes and Objects, Matrices Numbers, and Letters and Sentence Verification. Thus, these tasks improve reading as well as comprehension. However, despite this input there still may be some children whose comprehension of the text remains poor. These children are then termed as 'poor comprehenders'.

Once the mastery of phonetics has been attained, the attention is given to building the association between letters and sounds to make words and sentences. A useful method to make it clear is to break down the word to each syllable like m/a//t/. Another method, which is a reverse technique, first teaches the whole word and then breaks it down. This makes the recognition of sounds of the syllables easier to follow (SRA Basic Reading Program, Merrill Program).[3] Yet another method teaches the whole words with the help of visual aids, and bypasses the sounding out process (Bridge Reading Program).[4] The Multisensory Approach uses the combination of teaching whole words with the tracing technique (Fernald Method), so that kinaesthetic stimulation takes place while the child is reading.[5]

Whichever method is used, the aim is that the child should acquire reading skills. Once the phonetics—the association between syllable sounds to form words—is well established, then rhythmic series can be taught. For example, the 'at' series could run by prefixing the alphabet with 'at'. So, the series would run like this mat, hat, fat, rat, cat, etc. Similarly, the 'et' series would be pet, met, set, get. Akin to these, other word series can also be taught. Start with a simple series and as the child grows older, more complex ones can be taught. This takes care of the spellings as well.

Word Families

ab	ad	am	an	at
cab	bad	dam	can	cat
nab	cad	ham	fan	fat
crab	dad	jam	man	hat
drab	had	ram	pan	mat
grab	lad	slam	ran	pat

Figure 12: Sample of Word Families

As the decoding technique is understood and incorporated, expose the child to as many words as possible, so that those words become part of the vocabulary. Once the core vocabulary is achieved, expose the child to irregular words to increase reading accuracy. A regular reading habit and listening attentively while someone reads, increases both fluency and speed. This can be done by using the tracking method. This method is useful only with older children. It requires tracking the sentence after the speaker, so that correct pronunciation, attentive listening and correct syllables are learnt. It is a difficult method and should be used with confident children only.

However, as stated above, only learning to read is not sufficient. Comprehending the text read is also of vital importance. Before beginning a new chapter, try teaching conceptually important vocabulary that is those core words that are important to understand a particular topic or subject. For example, the chapter on plants may have important concepts like root, stem, flower, spores, photosynthesis, and so on. Once the lesson has been read, explain in detail what it is all about. Then go over the difficult words for understanding, meaning and spellings. Then ask questions, both implicit and explicit that cover the content. While reading remediation is going on, spellings can be taught as well, so that the logic of phonetics is clear to the child.

Both parents and teachers should encourage: the reading habit in children; playing word games like scrabble and hangman; and, learning the use of the dictionary.

Written Expression

Written expression encompasses two areas, spellings and sentence writing. Both these areas are linked to grammatical rules. Poor written expression is seen concomitantly with reading disorder. Hence, as mentioned above, learning of phonetics and phonemes would help in remediation of spellings and sentence writing.

The age-old methods of learning spellings are useful. Breaking the words down to the individual syllable sounds help to pick the spellings. To illustrate, the earlier example given for the word 'understanding', the syllabic combination would be un/der/stand/ing. The syllabic sounds make it easier to remember and, of course, repetition and constant practice benefits retention.

Traditional method of doing corrections, i.e., writing the misspelt word five times, is another useful method to acquire spellings. Overlearning is being used here. With young children the practice-by-play method is advisable. Words can be written with crayons, paint or colour pencils rather than a black lead pencil. Sand or mud can also be used as a variant to paper and pencil especially with a resistant child.

For any remediation work, try to make the task simple and achievable. Every child needs challenges to be motivated to study. However, too difficult text may appear as an unattainable goal to the child, which demotivates them. Conversely, too easy text, does not arouse interest. So, a short list of words, interspersed with variable difficulty level (some difficult and some easy words) would be learnt more enthusiastically than all difficult or all easy ones.

Try to cluster words that have some similarities. For example, you can keep in mind the length of the words, the beginning and ending of the words. Like all words ending in 'all'—such as, hall, ball, fall, gall, tall—can be clubbed together. As the child sees that some words are spelt alike, except for the first letter, the natural rhythm of the word aids remembrance. Sometimes the child tends to misspell a particular word even after being taught it umpteen times. For example, if the child spells 'duke' as 'duck', then write 'd' and 'k' in black ink and 'u' and 'e' in blue or red colour. The distinction of colours also is an adjunct to memory.

ust	ight	ouse	ist	ting	Ent
bust	light	house	mist	boosting	bent
dust	might	mouse	fist	dusting	cent
gust	night	douse	gist	jousting	dent
just	bright	louse	list	painting	lent
must	fright	rouse	grist	lamenting	tent

Figure 13: Spelling Families ending with

br	con	st	th	pr	sh
bright	concert	stand	think	prank	shot
brought	concise	straight	thought	prick	shoe
bring	console	stork	thing	prude	shock
bread	converse	study	thick	pride	shop
broad	confusion	story	thin	prance	ship

Figure 14: Spelling Families starting with

Sentence writing requires regular practice. One of the best ways to improve expression is to encourage the child to do creative writing, like writing essays or paragraphs. Some helpful ways are to prepare a short paragraph with some words missing that the child needs to fill in. This aids the direction of the story and gives the child an idea of how to frame a paragraph sequentially. If the teacher feels sufficiently satisfied with the progress of paragraph writing, then some key words can be given which the child uses to build a 5-line story. Slowly, the number of words can be increased.

Comprehension exercises where the child needs to answer questions based on the given paragraph is also useful. Reading structured text and answering the questions gives the child a fair idea how to do creative writing. Preferably, for creative writing, the child should be given topics that they can relate to easily and are age and grade appropriate.

These creative writing exercises cannot be for more than 15–30 minutes. To ensure that the learning is reinforced you can ask the child to prepare shopping lists, write letters to relatives, imaginary friends, pets or write in a diary. In case the facility of lending library is available, encourage extra reading and writing from books other than the course books.

Writing

Spellings and sentence construction remediation would be incomplete if attention is not paid to the writing ability of the child. We already know that the child's writing is messy and shoddy, letters do not sit on the line, words are cramped with little spacing, and speed of writing is slow. They also have an unusual grip while holding the pencil. Sometimes the child holds the pencil near the tip.

Before the remediation process starts, we have to work on certain basic aspects. The prerequisite of writing are coordination of eye and hand, grasp and strength of fingers, 'preferred hand' whether left-handed or right-handed, and general motor coordination.

To gauge eye-hand coordination, the ability to track the movement of the hand with the eye needs to be increased. Use a dark room and two torches. Move your torch slowly around the room and ask the child to track the light with his/her eyes. The child can also trace lines up and down, right and left, horizontal and vertical. The rationale behind these exercises is that the eye should learn to move smoothly along the direction of the hand. Variations of this technique can be used to increase the eye-hand coordination. To ensure general motor coordination, encourage skipping, hopping, jumping, running, balancing and cycling.

By the age of 7–8 years the handedness, i.e., the hand the child prefers to use, becomes clear. Please **do not** change the child's natural orientation as the brain gets confused because of mixed laterality (lack of consistent use of one side of the body, right or left, for most tasks).

For the left-handed child, the position of the paper should be under the left arm, and while holding the pencil, the left hand should be touching the paper directly in line with the little finger and wrist. The child's back and head should be slightly curved towards the right side. In case you do not find this then it is an indication that probably the child is yet not matured enough to start writing work.

To correct the unusual grasp of the pencil, certain activities that require holding and gripping may help the child. To rectify holding the pencil at the tip, a rough marker like a rubber band could be helpful. To lessen the painful grip, some exercises to strengthen the shoulder and hand muscles would be fruitful. To develop strength in shoulders, exercises can include pull-ups on swings and gymnastic bars or rings. To strengthen hand muscles, gentler exercises could be to squeeze clay dough, rubber ball, wet clay to mould different figures, or any other similar material.

Remediation needs to start with a practice session of writing alphabets both in capital and small letters. Start with small letters. The Montessori method follows this pattern:

- Set one: c, m, a, t
- Set two: s, r, i, p
- Set three: b, f, o, g
- Set four: h, j, u, l
- Set five: d, w, e, n, k
- Set six: q, v, x, y, z

In another method, small alphabets particularly are taught on four levels, depending upon the ease with which the child is able to pick up writing. These are based on the basic use of straight, horizontal, slanting and circular shapes which make up the English alphabets.

Writing Series
Small Letters a-z
Level 1: l, t, i, v, w, x, y, z
Level 2: h, n, m, r, j, u, f
Level 3: c, a, d, q, g, o, e
Level 4: b, p, s

The logic behind each level is to teach the child that the letters follow a pattern. Level 1 has alphabets made up of straight lines, either vertical (standing line), or horizontal (sleeping line), and a few have slanting lines. The alphabets are l, t, i, k, v, w, x, y and z. All the alphabets sit on the line, except for y which goes below the line.

Level 2 uses both the straight lines (as Level 1) and simple curved lines. This requires drawing straight lines and connecting them to a curved line. These include alphabets like h, n, m, j, r, u and f. Here f and h go above the line whereas j goes below. The rest sit on the middle line.

In Level 3, the curves of c are used. These are a little more difficult compared to earlier levels. The curved line with straight line combination is taught. These include the alphabets c, a, d, q, g, o and e. Here, d crosses the line upwards whereas q and g go downwards. The rest sit on the middle line. The child requires a good eye-hand coordination to be able to learn this.

The fourth level is the most difficult to master. Here the c is used by inverting it—as seen in b and p—or completing curving it as seen in s. Here b crosses the line upwards, whereas p goes downwards.

A third equally effective method to teach is by pattern drawing. In case the recognition of the alphabets has still not taken place, then teach according to the shapes required to write the alphabets. Start with pattern 'o' or circle shape which would include alphabets like c, d, o, a and g. Then go on with straight lines or pattern 'l' which will have the corresponding alphabets, i, l, k, f, t and j. Similarly, the pattern 'v', with corresponding alphabets of v, w, x and z; pattern 'n' with alphabets n, m, r, h, b and p. Pattern 'u' with alphabets u and y, and lastly pattern 's' with the alphabet s.

Always start with lower case (small) alphabets as the child sees these more often than uppercase or capital letters. Preferably cursive style should not be taught to the child with LD.

Apart from these patterns, let the child practise different shapes like circle, triangle, square, rectangle, semi-circle, star, cross and the plus sign. The more the practice of various angles, the quicker the child will grasp the concept of patterns related to writing.

Both teachers and parents can play games that help the child to practise the taught alphabet. Other than notebooks, many alternatives like wet clay, blackboard and chart paper can be useful. Even at home, chart paper can be pasted on the wall at the child's height to be used for practice. Tracing an alphabet with your finger on the child's back is another play method. Initially four ruled line notebooks should be used, so that the child learns to sit the letters within the lines. Gradually introduce the child to two-line notebooks.

If the child is resisting writing, then do not compel the activity. Again, alternative techniques need to be used. Encourage finger painting, as dappling in paint is a fun experience for most children thereby increasing the desire to hold the pencil. Above all, praise and encourage the child for every attempt made.

Mathematics

Children, by and large, find mathematics difficult and those with LD may find it more so, though it is not necessary that they do. Many children may have only dyscalculia. Some children may have mathematical difficulty where reading and comprehending the question may be the issue, and not computation. This is seen with many children who have severe dyslexia. In such cases only teaching computations may not be good enough. Word problems and problem-solving activities are more helpful. However, whichever technique is used, mathematics can only be mastered by daily practice. The concept of overlearning is best seen here. Repeated practice ensures that the logical steps to solve mathematical problems and tables remain with us for life.

Since those with LD find it problematic to grasp mathematical concepts—addition, subtraction, multiplication, division, remembering multiplication tables, fractions and telling time—the judicious use of visual aids, flash cards, computer games and workbooks, all help. Concrete apparatus can be number squares, multiplication squares, counters, coins or even beads—these can be used to explain the mathematical concepts of simple addition, subtraction, multiplication and division. Rote learning of multiplication tables also is fruitful. Remember visualization is a strong aid to learning. Multisensory methods—if used for short periods of time several times in a day—can recapitulate the previous learning.

The words that are used in mathematics need to be explained to the child, as mathematical vocabulary is different. Words like even-odd, order, place, point, log table, root table, all have a different connotation in mathematics. To support the learning, a simple mathematic lexicon or word list defining these terms can be given. Any such lexicon, if it is illustrated by diagrams or pictures, would aid memory functions as well as prove useful in grasping the concept.

To reinforce mathematical concepts make them part of everyday activity—such as counting steps; moving backwards and forwards as part of subtraction and addition concept; counting the number of notebooks collected in class, cutlery and plates at home, grocery items and so on. Multiplication and division too can be taught in similar fashion. For example, count 16 beads and ask the child to distribute the beads amongst 4 persons. See what technique the child adopts to distribute the beads. If the whole process is by trial-and-error method, then the child needs help. The simplest way would be to place one bead for one person, in this way making four piles. These methods are time-consuming, but the clarity of the concept is better. Later the child could be shifted to mental calculations. These methods help the child to overlearn a concept without the burden of book learning.

Some play methods for mathematics can be counting games, like dominoes, snakes and ladders, ludo, cards and monopoly. Since mathematical concepts are basically dealing with measurements, space and time, the child needs to learn to relate these phenomena to each other and in relation to everyday life. These everyday experiences, therefore, gain importance, as teaching mathematics only from books is rhetorical while this is practical.

Learning Strategies

No single learning strategy can be said to be the ultimate method of teaching. However, some strategies that adolescent students can use are: the SQ3R method, the Cornell method of making notes, and Mnemonics.[6, 7]

The SQ3R in its complete form is Survey, Question, Read, Recite and Review. Before starting any study, it is prudent to *survey* what one needs to read. The method is similar to having a rough map in mind before starting a venture. *Question* requires a rough estimate of questions related to the topic. The more questions you have about the topic the ready desire to seek answers to them. *Read* requires reading the text with understanding. In case illustrations, tables or any other visual adjuncts are given in the text then effort has to be made to go through them conscientiously. Children with LD, as mentioned earlier, tend to comprehend and remember better when visual aids are given. *Recite* requires repeating the read material periodically, especially the facts or text that are underlined as important. Going over the illustrated parts of the chapter several times would further reinforce learning.

Review requires going over to check what is really learnt. *It is not to check what all remains to be done.* It helps in mental revision and gives an idea to the teacher which are lesser remembered or comprehended portions. Such text may require clearer understanding and repetitions. Normally this should be done immediately after finishing a segment of the chalked-out material.

Cornell's method of note taking focuses on the 5Rs—Record, Reduce, Recite, Reflect and Review. **Record,** is the usual taking down of notes while the teacher is teaching. **Reduce,** is to condense the facts so that they can be represented by a single word or cue. **Recite,** is repetition of what has been written down. **Reflect,** as the word suggests, requires reflecting on the subject so that it is mentally revised again and not forgotten due to disuse. **Review,** requires going through the notes before starting with the next section of text.

Mnemonics is an old method of giving a name to each alphabet, so that each letter is a cue to remembrance.

Dealing with Attention Deficit and Directionality

Attention Deficit and Hyperactive Disorder and Attention-Deficit Disorder are both associated with LD. As children with ADHD grow up, hyperactivity normally reduces but attention deficit remains which is termed as ADD. In ADHD and ADD the attention deficit is common which requires dealing with: a) distractibility; b) span sustainability; and c) ability to concentrate for the required task to be completed. But, in ADHD, the associated factor of hyperactivity has to be dealt with as well.

In case the child has been diagnosed with ADHD and the condition is moderate to severe, attention sustaining exercises are not very effectual. The first line of treatment would be psychopharmacological. Once hyperactivity is better controlled and the child can sit long enough to complete a task, then these activities are beneficial. The activities can be of the following types:

1. Colouring
2. Sorting tasks
3. Cutting and pasting
4. Collage
5. Cancellation exercises
6. Jigsaw puzzles
7. Computer games

Colouring and sorting exercises are designed for the younger age group, whereas the others are designed for the 8+ age group. There are two rationales on which these exercises are constructed, namely precision and interest. Precision work requires more attention than routine work. If a task is interesting and favoured by the child, there is far more chance of holding its interest and the task being completed. Hence the activities are created keeping both these aspects in mind.

1. **Colouring tasks:** This is a simple way to engage a child. One can use either an illustrated drawing book or one can draw a figure for the child to colour. Another convenient method is to draw a square covering three-quarters of the page and ask the child to colour it. The next day, on a fresh sheet, draw a line in the centre of the square and let it be coloured by two different colours. Third day increase the difficulty, by adding two lines thereby making three columns. Next day, put a cross inside the square making a quadrangle. In this way continue increasing the difficulty level. One needs to take care of time allotted to complete the task. Normally 10 minutes for older children and 15 minutes for younger children should suffice.

2. **Sorting tasks:** This is again a play method. All the toys are gathered. A concept is given according to which the child needs to sort the toys. For instance, if the concept is colour, and say red colour is given. The toys that are red in colour must be chosen by the child. This is a brief 2–5 minutes exercise, the time depending upon the age. Younger children are given more time. One can use playing cards, WWF cards, toys, blocks, coloured beads, miniature animals, plastic flowers, different sized coins, pictures of birds and animals. Any material can be used that holds the interest of the child. DO NOT use the same material repeatedly, because inattentive children tend to tire easily and become bored.

3. **Cutting and pasting:** First give a theme that interests the child, for example cricketers. Then help to select pictures of cricketers from old newspapers or magazines. Draw a square frame round the picture, to be cut along the line by the child. The pictures can be pasted in a scrapbook or chart paper. Besides attention, this task increases the dexterity of fingers.

4. **Collage:** These same pictures can also be used for making a collage.

5. **Cancellation exercises:** Old newspapers can be handy for this exercise. Mark a small paragraph, consisting of at least 10 lines. Give a vowel or a consonant to cancel. For example, if you have asked the child to cancel 'm', then all 'm's' need to be cancelled in the selected paragraph. Please note the time taken for the child to complete the task. Then check for errors. There will be errors of omission (not cancelled the 'm'), errors of commission (cancelled alphabet other than 'm'). This exercise needs to be given every day, as it takes but a few minutes to complete. Change the alphabet every day.

6. **Jigsaw puzzles:** Normally most children do have jigsaw puzzles. Joining the pieces correctly in a fixed time, helps to sustain attention. Since no school or home can have an unlimited supply of jigsaw puzzles, one method is to cut pictures from newspapers and magazines into various pieces. One can continue making new puzzles, and as complicated as possible, by increasing the number of pieces to join.

7. **Computer memory games**: There are innumerable memory games on computers. One game per day would help in both attention and memory functions. Time to

complete the task and strict discipline to computer time must be maintained.

Teaching Directions: Left and Right

Since children with LD have difficulty in differentiating between left and right; struggle to read topographical maps; tend to reverse both alphabets and numbers; and can have mirror imaging—it is imperative to teach them directionality. Frequently, play methods are used as they are easy and fun for the child.

The child can wear a band on one hand to differentiate right and left. Games like 'Queen of Sheba' or 'I spy' can be modified for teaching directions, as one can say, 'Bring the pillow from the left side of the room', or 'Touch flowers kept on the right side of the room'. Please remember that the child and you should be facing the items from the same side. You can draw arrows pointing in different directions and ask the child to name the direction. Just be innovative and create such activities. Once directionality is learnt, then generalization to alphabets and numbers is easier.

Psychotherapies

None of the above work will be effective if the child is emotionally disturbed. As we have seen, most children with LD do have some associated problems. These need to be rectified simultaneously while remediation work is going on. Some of the therapies that are beneficial are Play Therapy, Behaviour Therapy, Cognitive Behaviour Therapy and Supportive Psychotherapy.

Play Therapy

Play therapy is a powerful therapeutic method for children aged between 3–11 years.[8] Play is considered a natural way for children to communicate with others, express their emotions and resolve any psychosocial issues. It helps them to be more socially integrated, decrease aggression and anger, develop social skills and coping behaviours, learn to empathize and regulate their emotions, and deal with their trauma.

There are two types of play therapy, directive and non-directive. In directive therapy the clinical psychologist plays a significant role, as the child has to be guided through play to bring about faster healing. Many types of mechanisms are used, namely storytelling, puppets, toys and sand trays. The child is guided during the play, helped to manipulate the toys or actively participate in storytelling to resolve the trauma or conflict.

The goals of non-directive therapy is the same, only that the clinical psychologist plays a more passive role. It is an unstructured play therapy with the underlying principle that, left free to express themselves, children learn to resolve their traumas and find their own solutions. Both types are effective.

Behaviour Therapy

Behaviour therapy is an umbrella term for a variety of therapies, based on learning principles. The rationale behind these therapies is that behaviours which have been learnt can also be unlearnt and new behaviours learnt in their place. Hence, the maladaptive behaviours are identified, targeted and then changed. There are many techniques developed, based on the learning theories of conditioning, both classical and operant (discussed in Chapter 2 on Learning Concepts). There are innumerable behaviour therapy methods, but I will describe only those that are relevant for treatment of children with LD.

Relaxation techniques: Amongst several relaxation techniques, progressive deep muscular relaxation is particularly helpful in relaxing tensed muscles. It was introduced by Edmund Jacobson in the 1920s.[9] The cue lies in the word 'progressive', which indicates that small groups of muscles are relaxed one at a time. The technique followed is of deliberately tensing the muscles and then relaxing them, thereby bringing the body to a low arousal level. The contrast between tension and relaxation is learnt, which helps a person to voluntarily relax themselves in tense situations. This is helpful for older children, especially anxious ones.

Systematic desensitization: Developed by Wolpe in 1958, systematic desensitization is based on classical conditioning theory.[10] The therapy has three stages. In the first stage an 'anxiety hierarchy' is made. In the second stage, the mechanism response is learnt. The third stage involves connecting the feared stimulus to the incompatible response, also called counter-conditioning. This method is effective in treating children with school phobia or school refusal.

With the child's help the anxiety hierarchy is made, which lists the least feared to most feared element of the school. Then the child is taught relaxation technique or coping mechanisms that could help in relaxing voluntarily. Gradually the child is exposed to the least feared situation about the school to the most feared one, but in the presence of a situation that is diametrically opposite to the feared one. For example, if the fear is of the peer group, then the child is exposed to the situation in the company of friendly students. In this way slowly but assuredly the fear related to school is overcome.

Contingency contract: This is a formal written contract between two or more persons that involves both rewards and punishments related to specific behavioural change. The contract has five specific tenets. The first step is to define what each person will *get*, if the desired behaviour is successfully completed. The second step requires *monitoring* of the behaviour. The third step involves meting out of *pre-agreed punishments*, if the desired behaviour is not being performed. In the fourth step, a person complying with the approved behaviour is given *bonuses*.

The behaviours—both the approved and disapproved ones—need to be documented. This documentation is to be used as *feedback* and it helps in deciding how much the reinforcers are earned as part of the fifth step. The 'contingency contract' method can be universally used for any kind of unacceptable behaviour as the method is fairly effective.

Token economy: In the 'token economy' method, reinforcement is given to the approved behaviour, by giving tokens that can be exchanged for a desired reward. For children, tokens can be substituted with different coloured stars. The colours could represent the points earned. After a specific number of stars are earned, the child can exchange them for a desired reward. This method is efficacious for motivating a child.

Cognitive Behaviour Therapy of CBT: This was Beck's way of treatment with distorted thoughts that caused mental problems.[11] CBT is grounded in the belief that the person's perception of the event, and not the event per se, is responsible for how the person will think, feel and react. As an illustration, if the belief is that nothing will go well, the child or adolescent will selectively pick up only those events that will reinforce this thinking. A constant reinforcement of this kind generates a negative belief system. Over a period of time, this cycle of negativity becomes the root cause of anxiety and depression. With CBT, these distorted thoughts are challenged and the evidence to counter the distorted thoughts are picked from the child's or adolescent's life history; CBT is more effective with older children and adolescents.

Supportive psychotherapy: This therapy is an adjunct to other psychotherapeutic methods. It is helpful in strengthening defences, maintaining control and restoring adjustment of a person. Some supportive methods are Guidance, Tension Control and Release, Environmental Manipulation, Externalization of Interests, Reassurance, Prestige Suggestion, Pressure and Coercion, Persuasion and Ventilation. With children some of these methods are useful.

i. *Guidance:* is one of the foremost methods used. Guidance means giving active help to the child. Here the therapist or counsellor or special educator is the directing authority who plans the daily regimen and allows no time for either idleness or destructive thoughts. Work or daily schedules are made, so that the child has ample idea as to what activity needs to be done within what time. This makes the child's time organized and gives him or her adequate time to study, play, socialize, indulge in hobbies, eat and sleep.

ii. *Externalization of interests:* This is the most often used method. The child is encouraged to take up alternative activities, particularly hobbies, recreational activities and creative arts. These include art, music, dance, drama therapy and diary writing. The basic aim behind these modes of therapy is to release pent-up emotions, gain confidence, learn coping mechanisms, socialization and to relate to the peer group and the environment in a positive way.

a) *Art therapy:* The emotions are expressed through creative activity. Depending upon the inclination of the child, colours, pencils, charcoal or crayons are used with specific encouragement for finger painting.

b) *Music therapy:* It is soothing for ruffled emotions, and if the child has an inclination to learn and perform on the stage, it acts as compensation for lack of academic success. Ditto is the relevance of *dance therapy.*

c) *Drama therapy:* This is a powerful therapeutic device for children who are traumatized, have inner conflicts, difficulty in relating to others and are unable to express themselves. Role-playing encourages the child to emote and overcome the conflicts. Children who face hostility from family members, school and peer group, are able to release the frustration, anger and counter hostility better.

d) *Diary writing:* This method is meant for older children and adolescents. Encouragement is given to pour one's feelings into the diary, hence it is also termed as an *'emotional diary'.*

iii. *Reassurance:* This proves extremely helpful for children who are depressed or anxious. Verbal reassurances that target the regaining of confidence in one's abilities are given. The emphasis is more on overall growth and not on academics. The aim is to divert the child's mind from self-doubting thoughts, ease anxiety and guide them towards self-improving mechanisms.

iv. *Environmental manipulation:* This requires bringing about a change in the child's situation, in case there are too many conflicts and hostilities. Though this is uncommon, but in case the hostility and conflicts have resulted in deteriorated mental condition of the child, then physical removal is the option. The child may be placed in foster care so that environment is congenial and pleasant.

v.   *Persuasion*: This aims to motivate the child to recognize the power within self. An appeal is made to the person's intelligence and reasoning ability. This is more effective with adolescents.

vi. *Ventilation*: This is a powerful method to alleviate the emotional baggage the child may be carrying within self. The child is encouraged to release pent-up emotions, conflicts, worries and anxieties. This again is meant more for adolescents. Children vent out through methods described above.

Family Therapy

The family needs to be involved while treating a child, especially where the members appear frustrated or angry or upset with the child. Parents also may suffer from low mood or even be depressed. In case parents are suffering from emotional disturbance themselves, they need individual psychotherapy. If the hostility towards the child is high, then the entire family needs to be involved in the session. Mostly a few sessions of counselling with the parents suffice.

These are some psychotherapeutic methods that we use in our daily practice. However, my job would remain incomplete if I do not have a special word for parents and teachers, who are the main persons in a child's life. The next two chapters are devoted to them to know how best to render help to a learning-disabled child.

8
A Note for Parents

'Between what is said and not meant, and what is meant
and not said, most of love is lost.'

–Khalil Gibran

IN AN IDEAL world, ideal parents ideally would know their children the best. However, it is equally true that neither is there an ideal world, nor ideal parents. Most parents do try to give their best to their children, whether giving roots or wings or unconditional love. Some parents make parenting their life goal, more mothers usually, as there are cultural, social, self and peer demands. Fathers conventionally have been less so inclined, as traditionally the role of child rearing had been allocated to mothers. Though in recent years, there has been an archetypal change with more and more fathers becoming actively involved in care-giving for their child.

Parenting children at any age is not an easy task. Each age puts diverse type of demands and pressures on the parents. This requires parents to dive into their reservoir of capacities—be it physical, emotional, mental, financial, social or cultural—to bring out solutions. Nonetheless, each such dive does not empty the reservoir, as it simultaneously fills up with the biggest asset called 'experience'. Each experience adds to the repertoire of coping mechanisms to deal with the ever-increasing problems.

Experience makes us aware of what each child's needs, wants and desires are likely to be. What may perhaps be a need for one, may be a constant demand for the second and a total rejection for the third. For the first child, parents are more experimental, whereas second and subsequent children are brought up with the experience gained while handling the first. As parents, the more we understand the emotions and feelings of the child/children, the further we walk towards the first step of positive parenting.

Parents' Involvement

Dhruv first met me when he was 8 years of age. He belonged to a well-to-do family. The family consisted of his father who ran a business, mother a teacher, an elder sister who was an above-average student, and grandparents. They lived in a big industrial city. In my first interaction I saw a shy but rather naughty child with bright eyes. The mother told me that he was facing problems in academics as it seemed that he was not inclined to study. The description given matched more of ADHD than LD. However, when I gave him a piece of paper and asked him to write his name, he reversed the D of his name. Immediately the mother complained that he still had not learnt to write his name despite being in Class III. This required psychoeducation for the mother about LD, and the need to assess him. We then went ahead with the testing.

The findings of the tests indicated that he was severely dyslexic, with an IQ of 123 that indicated superior intelligence. He had marked difficulty in reading, writing, mathematics and composition writing. In fact, his writing seemed like ancient manuscripts where you know that something is written but is not quite decipherable. The mother was briefed on how to handle his academics, his emotions and self-esteem as he was bound to face problems in school. I also encouraged the mother to share this information with the rest of the family, so that everyone would lend a helping hand. She left with the enigmatic words, 'Let's see'.

I met Dhruv again after 2 years. The once naughty and bright eyes were now dull and tense. He vaguely remembered me, and my hello was greeted from behind his mother's back. I sent Dhruv to sit in the adjacent room attached to my consulting chamber accompanied by his sister. I then asked his mother to brief me about the happenings of the intervening years. She updated an appalling story of Dhruv's academics being handled at home.

When she reached her hometown, her in-laws and husband refused to believe that the child had any disability. She and Dhruv were accused of having a non-serious attitude towards academics. She, in fact, faced physical abuse from her husband for sparing the rod and spoiling the child and then making an excuse for the child's non-performance. The grandfather and father both decided to take a hand in Dhruv's education.

As soon as the child returned from school, he was given a reprieve of half-hour to change his clothes and eat his lunch. He then had to sit with his grandfather to study mathematics. For every mistake he was caned. This continued for two hours every day. Again, a break of thirty minutes was allowed and then his mother had to help him complete his homework. The mother-in-law would sit in the same room to keep an eye on them. Another two hours of studies were expected to be completed. By this time the father would be back home. A third gruelling session of two hours with the father was accomplished for science, with frequent physical punishment.

The child's play time was scrapped and his favourite game, football, was discontinued. His one favourite leisure activity, television, was ruthlessly stopped, and any form of entertainment was denied to the child. The school had fared no better. He was treated harshly in school, as the father had requested that his son should be dealt with firmly if his work was not up to the mark. I was further told that the report I had given had not been submitted to the school by the father.

So now before me was a child who had not only LD, but an equal amount of emotional trauma. On an impulse I went to the room where he was sitting, absolutely subdued. I raised my hand to caress his cheeks and he flinched back expecting perhaps physical violence. Impulsively I hugged him, and he burst into noisy sobbing. I continued holding him till he subsided. I gave him some puzzles to solve and re-entered my chamber. I then asked the mother if her husband had accompanied her on this visit to her parents' house. When she affirmed, I asked her to call her husband to the hospital.

The father came albeit reluctantly. His first reaction was, 'Doctor, I do not believe in your diagnosis. The child is only naughty and needs a firm hand.'

So, I asked, 'How firm is firm?'

'Till he learns to obey.'

I further asked, 'His mother tells me that for two years you have been firm. How much firmer do you need to be before you are satisfied? And how much you have managed to help him gain academically?'

'Not much, but perhaps his mother is not making sufficient effort to teach.'

At that point I drew out Dhruv's previous protocols and some other protocols. I showed these protocols and pointed out the similarities in types of errors made by other children like reversals, type of spelling error and writing difficulty. The fact that other children with LD were showing similar signs made the father pause to think, if not being wholly convinced. I then gave him some standard write-up about LD and asked the parents to meet me the next day. I then reassured the child and sent the family home.

Initially I had a lengthy session with the parents and again explained about LD. Further, the associated conditions like ADHD and emotional turmoil that the children undergo, were explained to them. I also narrated the previous day's incident of Dhruv sobbing as if someone for once understood him, his flinching indicating his fear of punishment and the once bubbly and happy child, now showing abject lacklustre behaviour, looking defeated and helpless. I questioned them whether this was how they visualized their child's future, where mentally the child was broken just because academically, he was unable to cope? The mother too cried and blamed her in-laws and husband for Dhruv's condition.

At this juncture, I explained to the parents that LD remained lifelong but that did not mean the child would not be able to carve a career for himself. I quoted some famous names, which did reassure the father that the child's innate abilities needed to be encouraged to ensure a 'safe' and 'lucrative' (words that weighed with the father) career for his son. At the time of their leaving my chamber, I only cautioned them by these words, 'Love your child more than the child's academics.'

Parents are the best supporters and need to provide solace for their children in a hostile world. The amount of time and patience that the parents can give to their children nobody else can. Remember you can be one of the most inspiring agents to help your child.

Above I have shared the case of a set of parents who, particularly the father, were not willing to accept that their son had a disability. Nonetheless, there are many parents who are aware and accepting of the problem, but still feel powerless and helpless to ameliorate the situation for their child. Here, I will narrate another story which will help you to understand and perhaps identify how much the parents also feel distressed.

Shruti was a 12-year-old girl studying in an elite school. Her father was a successful businessman and her mother a homemaker. She had a younger brother who was academically brilliant. Since the beginning she was a below-average student. This made her a target for repeated scolding by the teachers. In every single class she was either reprimanded or sent to the principal's office as punishment. Since corporal punishment was prohibited in the school, she at least was saved from this ignominy.

Since recurrent admonishment was the norm with her, the class also started shunning her, fearing that perhaps association with her would deflect teacher's displeasure on them. Hence, by the time she was in Class III she had no friend to share her tiffin with, play with or talk to in the class. If she was absent no one would brief her or share their notebooks. Slowly, she moved from the first bench to the last bench, in one corner of the class.

The parents had initially approached me without bringing Shruti to the hospital. They wanted to know how best they could assist their child. The mother was particularly distressed, as Shruti was the first-born and a daughter, and they both shared a strong emotional bond. Every day, the mother would suspend all her social, home or any other engagements to help Shruti with her studies. Slowly, the entire household activities began to revolve round Shruti's academics. The parents would avoid any functions, festivals and social obligations so that their time and energies were not consumed needlessly.

Despite putting in so much of dedicated effort, the child's performance did not improve. Their anguish was apparent on their faces as they narrated these incidents to me. Since they had brought her notebooks, I went through them. It was quite evident that the child had LD. After explaining the nature of the disability, I requested them to bring Shruti to the hospital for testing.

Shruti was the textbook version of defeat and sadness. Her face never once broke into a smile. She had drooped shoulders and a stooping posture that almost gave the impression that for her the struggle was over, that she would rather hide in a corner and never venture out. During the interview Shruti reconfirmed what the parents had told me. There were two significant events that she added. She had repeated Class IV, so she was now with another set of students. In this class she did have a friend who was newly enrolled and had not been included in any class groups. However, the second event had further corroded her confidence, as she had found the new class equally rejecting and humiliating. In fact, she was bullied and teased by several names, 'loser', 'snafu' and 'dud'. Since her name began with the alphabet S, she was referred to as Snafu in her class.

Testing did confirm that she had LD. The poignant aspect was that neither the school nor the parents had recognized the problem and the child needlessly had suffered emotionally. Had the remediation teaching started earlier, the child would not have fared so badly.

I'm sure many parents would identify with the parents of Shruti. Many would recognize the upheavals that their children must have faced or are facing regularly in school and social gatherings. This is not an easy responsibility to shoulder. The situation is more burdensome when mothers are also employed. Thus, the pressures of employment, home, marriage and children all are amply served on the parents' plate, where perhaps none can be forsaken nor given up.

The liability increases when it is a nuclear family, as the joint family support is missing. Consequently, the onus and stress on the parents is much more. At the end of the day parents are also human beings with their own failings, fallacies, foibles, frustrations and fantasies. Hence dear parents, though easier said than done, even when there is a debacle in your lives please do not give up or feel unnecessarily defeated. Ups and downs happen in everyone's lives and need to be used as catalysts to reaffirm our resolutions.

Parental Stressors

Parental stress is multi-layered, multidimensional and multifold. Stress occurs from a multitude of reasons. Not only do the parents have to deal with the LD child's academic and emotional problems, but in case there is more than one child in the family, then demands of the other child or children need to be met as well. Most parents can cope with these demands, albeit with reservation and strain.

The next section is a glimpse of most frequently occurring stressors that parents face. This is only given to reassure you that you are not alone with these problems.

Effect of Stress on Emotions

Managing one's own emotions or that of the distressed child, is a prime challenge for parents, second only to the child's academics. Most parents report feeling exasperated and irritated while helping with the child's studies. They are faced by umpteen excuses for not sitting long enough to complete the homework. Some common excuses made are: 'I do not feel like studying', 'I'm too tired', 'I do not like the subject', 'What is the point, I'll forget it again', 'Teacher is not nice and scolds me so I will not study her subject', and so on and so forth. Occasionally such pretexts can be forgiven and overlooked, but constant whining is bound to be frustrating making the parent irritable and angry.

Parents do complain of physical tiredness and emotional saturation; the need to get away for some time, wishing someone could share their troubles. These reactions are due to stress. Thus, controlling or channelizing your own emotionality and the child's indifference, anxiety or naughtiness—whichever the case may be—could prove to be a major stressor.

Innumerable parents that I have met, complain of mood disturbances too. As often as children, parents also complain of being anxious and depressed. Most often it is not a major syndromal depressive episode, but dysthymia. Dysthymia is a low-level mood disturbance that has lasted for more than two years. This was seen in the mother of Shruti. She had literally shackled and isolated herself and Shruti, to devote herself entirely to Shruti's academic achievement. Pervasive anxiety is seldom seen in parents, but is palpably present during the child's examinations, class tests or public performances. Those parents who vicariously identify themselves with their children, are more prone to these upsets.

A self-created stressor amongst parents of children with LD is lack of acceptance of the problem and the subsequent resultant blame game played between them. As seen in the case of Dhruv's parents, there was denial of the diagnosis itself. Dhruv's father's reaction on being informed about the diagnosis was rather rough and inappropriate. Blaming the spouse for negligence or heaping culpability of generating the problem is not helpful. Not only in Dhruv's case, but in many others as well, I have seen parents pointing fingers at each other. Such reactions are neither beneficial nor constructive in addressing the concerned issue.

Geeta was an 11-year-old girl who was referred to me by the child neurologist as she had severe academic difficulty. She had been suffering from epilepsy since she was a few months old. Family history revealed that her maternal uncle and aunt suffered from epilepsy too. Since the first seizure, her father squarely blamed the mother for bringing the affliction into the house. He refused to hold or even touch the child. Since he was a rich man, he hired a nanny to look after the baby. The child and nanny were shifted to another part of the house. Hearing of the child's pitiable condition, the maternal grandmother took her away to her own house. A year later another daughter was born to the parents and subsequently, five years later, a son. Both children were free from epilepsy.

Whenever the children visited their maternal grandmother's house, the father used to caution them not to play, interact or even touch the eldest sister. Naturally there was no bonding between Geeta and her siblings. Unfortunately, the grandmother died when Geeta was 9 years old, and her happiness seemed to have vanished with her. She was back in her own home with her parents and siblings now. She was kept in another part of the house and was not allowed to mingle, play or eat with the rest of the family. Now she was grown up enough to realize the discrimination at home. The mother noticed that slowly Geeta was becoming withdrawn and looked sad not only at home but even in school, as reported by the teachers. Side by side her seizures re-occurred. Her mother then realized that the medicines for her seizures were being administered irregularly by the caregiver. Erratic timings and inadequate dosage had increased the frequency of seizures. When the mother tried to divide her time between the three children, it angered the father to the extent that he asked her to leave the house. She did so, taking the elder daughter with her.

A month after leaving the house, her son fell seriously ill. Since the father could no longer manage the children alone, he asked his wife to come back home. She agreed but with a rider that the eldest child would be treated at par with the other children. Reluctantly the father agreed.

On hearing this history, it was essential to psycho-educate the father about epilepsy, that it was neither infectious nor transferable. The relationship between epilepsy and LD was also explained. He was given some relevant literature to read as well. On regular follow-ups I saw the father accepting his first-born and all the three children bonding well with each other. Since both the daughters were now in *the same class but different sections I enrolled the help of the second sister to help the elder one. A special educator was hired by the father as well, so that Geeta could cope with the curriculum. So once the blame game was neutralized, a more effective and progressive attitude developed, bringing about conflict resolution in the family.*

Another immediate problem within the family can be sibling rivalry. Since each child is important and each has separate demands, it can be difficult for parents to manage. A substantial amount of time would be consumed in teaching the child with LD, as they require more time to learn, with elaborate explanations and repetitions. Patience is also tried while boosting flagging enthusiasm to learn; and when performance remains poor, then working closely with the child to give confidence can be time consuming. Other children may resent this exclusive time spent with one child alone. A parent told me that once her daughter, who was independent and brilliant academically, tore up her notes and refused to study as she was never the centre of attention.

A substantial number of parents mentioned that it was difficult to make the extended family understand the reason for poor performance of the child. Most mothers mentioned that they were blamed for being either overindulgent or non-caring towards their charges. Nevertheless, the situation tended to worsen when parents were unable to control or minimize unfair comparisons being made amongst the siblings, cousins and even neighbourhood children. Many parents felt embarrassed about revealing the poor marks attained by their child and at the same time also felt ashamed for letting their children down in others' presence. A few mothers were indignant about the unsolicited advice given by well-meaning family members.

Another dilemma faced by the parents is about getting their child labelled as dyslexic.

Veeru was 8 years old when I first saw him in the hospital. He had primary dyslexia. For several years he enjoyed benefits in the school given by CBSE. At the time of filling the Class X form for the board examination, his parents came to know that the final mark-sheet of the board examinations would carry the label of Persons with Disability (PwD). They asked me to certify that Veeru had no disability. I obviously could not do so. The parents decided not to attach the fresh report that was needed to be submitted with the filled form. The school was also annoyed by the parents' attitude. However, the child wrote the examinations without taking the benefits granted to LD students. Needless to say, the poor boy failed in every subject except Computers.

An issue related to the above case is the parents' predicament regarding choice of subjects, in case the child needs to drop the difficult ones for easier ones. Most parents, for reasons best known to themselves, prefer the academic Science stream, if not that, then, Commerce and, last of all, Humanities. Thus, if the child is unable to cope with either Science or Commerce, it becomes a major source of stress for parents. Many parents express their anxiety about the child's future career.

Archit was in Class X when I first met him. He had come for the certification for dyslexia that had to be submitted to the Board. The test findings suggested severe difficulty in mathematics, comprehension and reading. This indicated not only dyslexia but dyscalculia as well. However, the parents were insistent that Archit would take up the Science stream in Class XI. In fact, they told me that the father was concentrating on Science and Mathematics only, so that he scored well in these two subjects. Poor performance in the class tests did not bother them.

However, during the counselling session, I suggested to them to let him study equally for other subjects, otherwise his overall performance would be mediocre. Also, as dyscalculia was indicated on the tests, it would be preferable if they did not insist upon the Science stream. However, I came to know that none of this advice was heeded. I came across them accidently in the hospital, four months after the declaration of the results. Archit had failed in all subjects, so he had to repeat Class X. Nonetheless the undaunted parents were filling up the form for repeat examinations as a private student. He was being home-coached by the parents so that he could take up the Science stream in Class XI.

History was repeated, as he failed again.

These above examples show that parental stress centres round achievement in school, career and vocational choices, acceptance in college and university, expectations regarding earnings/ emoluments, future family life, and ability to be responsible for self and others. These parental concerns are genuine and serious, but not overwhelmingly insurmountable. Preferably, parents should aspire for their children prudently—based more on reality than on set social norms.

Most parents, particularly mothers, tend to sacrifice their careers, ambitions and social life, to labour alongside their children. Some mothers take it well, but many resent the lost opportunities and thwarted ambitions. They frequently begrudge the time spent at home, feeling tied down, cutting up their social life as their normal life is now governed by the school calendar, lack of respite and, in the end, disappointment of poor marks. Perplexity is also expressed about dealing with the child's behaviour. No single coping strategy seems to sustain for long. The coping mechanism that appears to motivate the child today, falls utterly flat the next time. The bewilderment is much more, when one consistently has to be innovative to deal with aberrant behaviour, as the child proves equally original in finding ways to avoid expectant behaviour. Many parents express a sense of helplessness, hopelessness and defeat.

I'm quite sure that most parents would have identified with the problems listed here. Nonetheless, this is not an exhaustive list of stressors that parents face. I have barely touched the tip of the iceberg. Needless to say, the idea here is to make parents aware that they are not isolated with unique problems, but that similar difficulty is shared alike by a multitude of parents. As parents, please do not feel disheartened, disappointed and helplessness, because proactive steps may substantially resolve the daily hassles you face. The idea should be centred around wholesome development of the child, so that he/she grows up into a self-respecting, confident and worthwhile member of the society.

Ensuring Adjustment by Bringing Changes in Self

The first step towards diffusing any stressful situation is to ensure adequate and healthy adaptation to the situation at hand rather than catastrophizing it. Whatever the academic challenges, the physical, mental and social life of the child needs to be as near normal as possible for better adjustment. Adjustment is the psychological process through which people manage or cope with the demands and challenges of everyday life. In other words, when a person is known to have a better fit with the environment, operates effectively within their social setting, is more oriented towards growth, forms durable relationships, is able to redefine relationships in a positive manner, is capable of dealing with stress and anxiety in a more reasonable manner, elicits positive feelings, switches to fresh goals that satisfy their own needs and behaves in a socially acceptable manner—this is termed as good adjustment.

Two other kinds of adjustments are imperative for the healthy growth of the child, namely, social and emotional. Social adjustment is the achievement of balance in social relationships, usually aided by the appropriate application of social skills. This would involve making friends, having the ability to get along with the peer group and a feeling of acceptance in society. Emotional adjustment refers to the maintenance of emotional equilibrium in the face of internal and external stressors. This involves acknowledging, accepting, adapting to and overcoming the adverse situation.

These are not impossible challenges. As parents you need to equip yourselves. The first step involves acceptance that there is a genuine problem. The child is not faking or being naughty or not applying himself/herself. This requires certain attitudinal changes in yourselves. Attitudes develop over time as we experience the world and form judgements. Thus, to change them also will take time. But as it is said, charity begins at home. Unless *you* change your attitude regarding the problem the child is facing, you will not take the necessary proactive steps to address the issue. Remediation teaching and tapping the potential, I believe, would be preferable to cursing one's fate or the youngster. Here are a few suggestions that may help you to tide over.

The foundation stone for any change that we plan is a transformation of our thought processes. This requires letting go of the negative thoughts. *Positive thinking does not mean thinking impossible goals or denying the difficulties,* but being realistic, assessing both the pros and cons, and working towards enhancing the pros while simultaneously reducing the cons. Drawbacks never fade from our lives, they only get partially covered by the positives. Hurts diminish because of the positives.

Some of the ways to enhance positive thinking would be by using CBT methods. By way of illustration, you can reframe negative thoughts by imagining the worst scenario and then also thinking of the best and what likely outcomes you can visualize in both types of situations. You may even maintain a diary to write down your alternatives to cope with difficult situations.

You can build a close and positive relationship with the school and with like-minded and similarly situated parents. Brainstorm with other parents to bring requisite changes for the benefit of the children. In case you are a non-working parent or can take time off from work, you can volunteer day-services as 'Mother as teacher', to the school. As far as possible, try to be in the company of people who remain positive in dire situations and are problem-solvers.

Positive thinking is further enhanced when the vocabulary that you use is also positive. The parents should label the child's actions with positive terms. To illustrate, instead of calling the child 'tiresome' they can term the child as 'energetic'. The terms 'slow' and 'sluggard' can be re-termed as 'taking a little more time'.

Negative vocabulary evokes negative emotions and disappointments.

Most parents do take it sceptically when I ask them to believe in the worth of their child. Since the child performs poorly in academics, the parents often have the belief that the child is good for nothing. This is not true. Those with LD have talents that remain buried under the academic weight. It is only with time and patience that one can discover what would be of interest to the child and can eventually be a source of livelihood too.

In case the child too is inclined towards academics, then emphasize the educational goals. If the child genuinely dreams of college education or entering some particular profession, *encourage* this thinking. I have dealt with several children who had clear-cut ambitions since their young age, but had dyslexia. The school years were difficult for the child as well as the parents.

One child had always dreamed of being part of NASA. To nurture his dream and to encourage the child to read, I asked the parents to buy illustrated books related to the subject. He did exceptionally well in science and mathematics throughout, because of the extra reading and knowledge that went beyond his years. And yes, today he is working in NASA.

Failure is a word forever hanging like Damocles's sword. Instead of letting the child feel the ignominy, try putting failures in perspective. One, or a few, disappointments should not be considered the norm. Emphasize on successes too; each success needs to be pointed out to the child. Yes, there should not be any scope for discouragement as every unsuccessful attempt is but a stepping-stone for a new beginning. Please quote examples of Edison who experimented innumerable times to make the bulb. As rightly pointed out by the late Denis Waitley, 'Failure should be our teacher not our undertaker.'[1]

As said earlier, your goals need to be realistic keeping in mind the amount of disability the child has and the time available to you. Naturally you would be required to juggle your time and perhaps give up the frequency of some of the enjoyable activities. Please do not allow resentment to build up. You can cope by simplifying tasks, particularly at home. If need be, learn to ask for help. In case help is not easily available, then just reduce the number of chores. Certain commitments or even social obligations cannot be ignored. So be realistic in choosing which to honour and which to refuse. Learn to say a polite no without offending your family, extended family and social acquaintances. But like Shruti's mother, do not become a social ostrich nor let the same fate befall the child.

No parent is superhuman. The tags super-mom and super-dad are really only tags. I have met innumerable parents who feel guilty at failure and blame themselves needlessly. Accept your own limitations and those of the child, instead of feeling stressed, depressed and anxious. As a family learn to laugh together and enjoy togetherness. Do have outings and holidays like any other household.

Physical rest is essential for both the parents and children. So adequate sleep and an exercise regimen should be part of your daily life. I have come across parents who would wake up at 3 or 4 a.m. to teach the child, when they themselves were sleepy and irritable and so was the child. This is an unnecessary burden and does not solve the purpose. Neither does the use and abuse of substances like alcohol, nicotine or even caffeine.

The parents who have a strong ability to organize, are better off. As far as possible, plan your day and the week. It need not be meticulously or religiously rigid but comfortably planned so that there are no unpleasant surprises. Even if there are unexpected happenings then organized parents can handle them well.

Helping the Child with Academics

The basic ground rule with LD is to use the concept of overlearning. Overlearning refers to practising any newly learnt skill beyond the point of initial mastery. This no doubt is effective, but requires a lot of patience and calmness. In case you are a short-tempered person, your anger will only lead to worsening of the child's performance and other psychological problems.

Certain groundwork you need to do with yourself before attempting to facilitate the child's academics:

i. Listen to the child's difficulties for they are genuine.
ii. Be tuned to the child's verbalizations as to the technique he/she finds useful and helpful.
iii. Consistent and regular teaching is most effective.

iv. Be in constant touch with the child's teacher and have regular meetings with him/her to devise new, better and effective teaching methods.

v. Do not expect to see a rapid change or improvement. Children with LDs take a longer time to learn.

vi. Seek outside professional help, particularly special educators, if you are unable to teach the child yourself.

vii. You will perhaps be the first persons to recognize any change in your child's behaviour. If you find consistent and pervasive changes in mood, anxiety or behaviour, then it is prudent to seek professional help immediately. Apart from being an impediment in academic progress, mental problems are obviously detrimental to the well-being of the child.

viii. Above all, learn to reward every good performance of the child. Do not bribe, but reward, good performance.

Facilitating Academic Learning: You already know the remediation techniques. In addition to them here are some of the things you can do at home.

i. Try to make the lessons simple and interesting.

ii. Break the lessons into small segments. Try to build association between the two segments that you have made. For example, if you are telling the child about plants then, if possible, physically show the plant to the child. *Children with LD learn faster once they have a visual image in mind.* This can be followed by labelling the various parts. You can at the same time, instruct about the functions of each part labelled. Generalization of knowledge about other fruits and vegetables associated with the type of plant you were teaching about, can now be built.

iii. If you follow a logical pattern of teaching, the child will feel less confused and will easily retain the concept taught. It is normally advisable to ask the child to repeat the concept immediately after being taught and again revise the next day. Revision by repetition is an age-old method.

iv. Be a source of information. Never give misleading information. Never evade questions that a child asks, for it dims natural curiosity.

v. Always have another set of books and workbooks so that the child can practice at home.

vi. Be tuned to the style of teaching the child is responding to, instead of just following the traditional method of teaching. For example, if the child can grasp the lesson being read out to him/her better, then read the lesson aloud. Ensure that the child's finger is tracing the word and sentence if you are reading the text aloud. This will ensure that the child is attentive, knows and remembers the pronunciation of the word.

vii. Use markers to underline important concepts.

viii. Structure the important study activities of the child. Try to maintain the timings, place of study and routine of the child.

ix. Think of all the ways you can help the child. If the child needs more diagrams and pictures to understand, then provide it.

x. Encourage the child to engage in co-curricular activities. Achievement in these activities boosts the morale, when positive strokes in academics are far and few.

xi. Make a point to keep the child informed of current affairs, as extra reading may not be possible. The child should not feel left out or be at a disadvantage in company due to lack of awareness of happenings in the world.

xii. Reward each effort with emphasis on direction and not on perfection alone.

xiii. Dear parents, never make comparison between your children. Each child is different and should be treated as a unique individual.

However, the story does not end here.

Be a back-up support to the teachers:

i. First and foremost, meet the teachers and find out what special measures are being taken to teach the child in school.

ii. Try to closely imitate the special teaching style being adopted by them.

iii. If the school authorities allow it, then sit in the classroom and see how the teachers are teaching.

iv. Especially learn how they are disciplining your child and children in general.

v. Request the teachers to hold frequent meetings, other than Parent–Teacher Meetings, to discuss the strategies and progress of your child.

How to give instructions:

i. While giving any instructions to the child try to use simple and short sentences. Lengthy sentences tend to confuse.

ii. Try to give one instruction at a time.

iii. See that the instructions are understood and followed.

iv. Reward every successfully carried out instruction by giving a hug or saying good or excellent.

v. You will also need to teach the child other self-help skills.

Allot responsibility:

i) Assign some regular responsibility at home, like making own bed.

ii) From early age assist the child to put the toys in their proper place. As the child grows older, ensure that it is their responsibility to: pack their bag, set out their uniform and polish their shoes—the tasks should be done in this order. Apart from cultivating a sense of responsibility, you are also ensuring self-pride and independence in the child.

iii) Teach a complicated activity, like making the bed in reverse order—first day start by spreading the bed cover. Next day, pillows are placed in position followed by spreading the bed cover. Third day, start by spreading the bedsheet and folding the blanket, placing the pillows in their right place and spreading the bed cover. In this way, the child learns something new besides learning the sequence as well.

iv) Persuade the child to participate in community services. These can be related to festivals, religious rituals or an hour on birthdays, with a visit to an orphanage or an old-age home. This increases their social participation as well as helps in being worthy citizens of the society.

Help the child to be organized:

i. Allot a specified place for every specific thing, be it books or toys.

ii.   If possible, provide shelves and not drawers so that the shelves can be marked by labels or pictures.

iii. Teach the child to place things neatly on the shelves. Demonstrate what you mean by 'neatness'.

iv.   The child's room should not be cluttered with extraneous household items.

v.   Try to follow a particular routine, like getting up and going to bed at a specific time, study or play time.

vi.   If possible, put up a small note for the things that the child is expected to do that day, as quite often the child tends to forget.

vii. Teach the child to maintain a diary for jotting down homework or any other expected work.

Formation of rules and inculcating expected behaviours at home:

i.   It is important to form rules at home for better clarity of expected behaviours and time management. Consistency, but not rigidity, should be the guiding factor.

ii.   While the child is studying, limit the use of noisome gadgets like television, laptops or videos. Even if one child has completed the studies, he/she should be engaged in another noise-free activity.

iii. A democratic household is far better compared to an autocratic one. Let the children participate while forming rules for running the house.

iv.   When the child decides his/her own punishments, the chances of adhering to the rules are higher.

v.   Let the child understand that breaking of the rules sometimes is not bad, but it should not happen too often.

vi. Avoid nagging and scolding as much as possible.

vii. When scolding for current misbehaviour, do not bring up any previous misdemeanours. Doing so will only worsen the situation.

viii. Let other siblings also follow the same rules. Quite often, either the other siblings look down upon the LD child or resent the attention given to the LD child. It becomes imperative to handle both the contemptuous feelings and the rivalry for attention. Be alert to notice which method works best for which child.

ix. At all costs let the child feel wanted and loved, despite the problem in studies. Never align yourself with anyone against your child, for it is one of the cruellest blows that any parent can give. Reprimand in private.

x. When you need to discipline or scold the child, always tell the reason for scolding and demonstrate the expected behaviour. When the child imitates that behaviour, show your pleasure.

xi. Help the child to be independent by encouraging them to make decisions. The worth of the decision is the process, rather than the feasibility or rationality. Slowly, as confidence is developed, guide the child towards making rational decisions.

xii. Try to form an association of parents whose children are facing similar problems. This will help you to be exposed to different techniques that have worked or failed. Also, such groups give emotional support to each other as well.

The above are some basic changes and guidelines that you can follow. They are neither exhaustive nor applicable in all cases. See which ones are beneficial and effective for you, the child and the rest of the family. The smoother the road the faster is the ride.

'If I accept sunshine and warmth, then I must also accept thunder and lightning.'

–Khalil Gibran.

Parenting is a combination of both.

9
A Note for Teachers

'The teacher who is indeed wise does not bid you to enter the house of his wisdom but rather leads you to the threshold of your mind.'

–Khalil Gibran

TRADITIONALLY, TEACHERS HAVE been regarded as fountains of wisdom and, at least in our country, are respected and revered. Since they give knowledge and are mostly an alternative parent figure in school, their role is of paramount importance. The help they can engender to the learning disabled is not limited to imparting education alone, but to a wider role of being a guide, role model and motivator.

Various institutes, organizations like CBSE and the Rehabilitation Council of India, have done a commendable amount of work in spreading awareness, training teachers or bringing about changes to ensure that children with LD remain in mainstream academics. So, dear teachers, I'm sure you must have some knowledge by now and do realize the importance of your role.

In Classrooms

The real challenge for the child as well as the teacher begins in the classroom. Since there are many children in a class it is difficult for the teacher to pay individual attention to a particular child. However, the difficulty is not so big if certain strategies are used.

Forming a Positive Attitude

The attitude of the teacher towards children with academic difficulty is of vital importance. Those teachers who are approachable, sensitive, understanding, non-threatening, non-judgemental, helpful and *willingly* listen to the child, are in an advantageous position. Such teachers inculcate a *desire to learn* in the child, without having to make undue efforts. This would be further amplified if occasionally the child is praised, hugged and patted on the shoulders by the teacher. When the teacher shows an interest in the progress of the child and is prepared to *talk* and is *ready to help*, it becomes more like a joint venture of the teacher and taught. A frank talk, an expressed understanding and steady assistance is likely to tap maximum potential.

How to Stop Humiliation, Both Intentionally and Unintentionally

As a teacher you may have to deal with certain hostilities and jealousies of other children in the class. Two kinds of issues may crop up. One, where the other children may feel that despite 'bad' work more attention is being paid to a particular child. Or conversely, they may become contemptuous and humiliate the child for needing more attention. You need to deal with both.

It has been astutely said by Khalil Gibran that 'to belittle you have to be little'. This wisdom should be part of the school training for all children, so that they desist being contemptuous and scornful of those less fortunate than them. Part of successful personality growth is the development of adult emotions of compassion, benevolence, sympathy, empathy, kindness and consideration for others.

Hence, as a teacher, you need to lead by example. Occasionally, nearly all students are scolded in the class, but the LD student may get repeated scolding. Avoid scolding, and never ridicule the child in front of the class, peer group or parents.

Another form of humiliation is displaying the notebook of the LD child as an example for the others not to follow. These children become the butt of jokes, bullying and teasing—especially when the teacher is absent from the class. Children who do want to be friends with the LD child may themselves feel scared or threatened with being similarly isolated by classmates.

Be careful how you punish or reprimand the child. Making the child stand in a corner or outside the classroom, calling the child frequently to your desk, criticizing their work severely, throwing their copies or even giving corporal punishment, can all be demeaning.

Try to avoid sentences such as, '*this is very easy; anyone can do it*'. Since it is not easy for the LD child, it becomes a self-depreciating experience—something to be feared and to feel ashamed about—to be the only one bereft of praise. It would be helpful if the child is praised for something in the presence of classmates, clapped for, a 'good' written on the note-book and said in front of others, or words to the same effect. This would enhance self-esteem and the desire to learn. Never, ever draw unhappy faces on their copies.

In case you catch or hear a child being bullied either physically or verbally, give a general talk to the class. However, if bullying persists then stricter action should be taken against the bullies, so that the target child is not further humiliated. Often such children refuse to attend school as there is nothing pleasant for them to look for in the class.

How to Motivate in Class

A word of encouragement from the teacher is always motivating for a student. In case the child is struggling too much with academics, encourage participation in extra-curricular activities to enhance confidence, self-esteem, sense of achievement and feeling of responsibility.

Reward the child frequently for good work. Reward can be tangible or intangible. Tangible can be giving a sweet, drawing a smiling face in the copy, clapping in class; and intangible could be verbal praise, making the child the class monitor for a day, calling the child to clean the board, or some such activities or responsibilities. The idea is to make the child feel included, responsible and a productive member of the class. Try never to single out the child either for reprimand or praise unless the situation warrants it. Scolding the class or praising the class with exceptions being pointed out is more helpful.

Try to have some element of surprise or new discovery that makes the lesson more interesting by giving examples from real life and showing working models. Set achievable standards that should include less written work and more oral work. Work needs to be doable and achievable in the allotted time. The idea is to make the child believe that academic targets are not impossible to accomplish.

Regularly give the child some responsibility related to the classroom, especially delivering messages. This helps in making the child more attentive, as you are infusing the art of rehearsing the messages to be repeated. A habit of rehearsing helps the child learn easily when remediation teaching takes place. Also, if the child is asked to repeat the message back, hearing their own voice becomes a useful aid to memory. For example, certain long words like 'message', 'delivered' get repeatedly rehearsed and they get fixed in the memory.

Involve the parents in a positive way, so that they too feel a part of the special programme designed for their child. Parents should not be made to feel guilty or disgraced for the problem. While speaking to them, do not label the child as learning disabled as that increases parental anxiety and in return may get transferred to the child.

How to Ensure Attention Sustenance

Every teacher knows that no two children are alike, therefore each child must be handled in a different way. One of the biggest tasks for the teachers is to adopt certain strategies to cater to each child's unique attentional needs, without letting the situation go out of hand.

The teacher must adapt according to the situation and the personality of the child. Children with LD are notoriously inattentive. As mentioned in earlier chapters, the co-morbidity of ADHD is present with most forms of LD.

Hence, it is wise to let the child be seated near you, preferably in the front row away from the door and windows. If the attention of the child is wavering, a stern look or touching the child's shoulder lightly will bring back the attention to you. Give the child that extra attention when it appears that there is some impediment in understanding instructions or beginning work. Help without creating and making a fuss. Preferably the child should work in a quiet and non-distracting environment. If that is a near impossibility, then use the above stated strategies.

Academic Assistance in Class

While reading: As by now you are familiar with the symptoms of LD, you know that children struggle with both reading and writing. Assistance would be required both academically and psychologically. I will try to cover most of both, which will act as guidelines to deal with the situation in the classroom.

Never ask the child to read a lesson aloud in the classroom situation when preparation is inadequate, for it will only increase anxiety and feelings of humiliation.

Allow the child time for self-assessment to gauge comfort level to read aloud. Do not hurry the child while reading, as they tend to lose the line and paragraph. They can be assisted by use of a footrule (ruler) or similar instruments to relocate the line. In case of hesitation, ask text-related questions so that speaking in class is not a formidable task.

However, if the child has read aloud in the class, words of encouragement and praise would make headway in boosting confidence. Assess performance more for oral than written work. Since writing is a problem, the assessment through only written work would be inadequate, as written work would have innumerable mistakes and may not be sufficient to assess the child's knowledge. Ask relevant questions to see how much text has been comprehended and reproduced.

The child is likely to be stuck over long words. Pronounce every word loudly, slowly and clearly so that the child can follow it. Read the word slowly, breaking the word into different syllables. For example, break a long word like understanding into un/der/stand/ing. Breaking the words makes it easier to read. Follow this with writing the same on the blackboard, so that the different recognizable syllables are retained by the child.

Do not give a long list of words to learn. Break the list into smaller lists so that it is easier to master the task without the child feeling fatigued. Try to grade the difficulty of the words, so that the list is in the ascending order of difficulty, that is, it starts from easiest to most difficult. For example, start by simple words like cat, hat, mat to more difficult ones like house, horse, etc.

A dictionary should not be used to teach *pronunciation*. As there is likelihood of not grasping the right consonant, it would only lead to confusion. Most children with LD pick up words orally much more easily and quickly than the written word.

Give new information more than once. Ask several children to repeat it in the class. If possible, *in private*, make the child repeat the lesson, both reading and spellings. If you lack time, then seek the parents' support to make the child practise at home.

While writing: Written work of a child with LD is generally shoddy. The child needs more time than the others to write even simple sentences and makes more mistakes than an average child. The child needs to be allowed to function at a comfortable pace.

While assessing the child's performance greater emphasis should be paid to oral rather than the written work. Mark the child's work on the content rather than on neatness or spellings.

Please *do not* use a red ink pen to check written work, because if the entire work is dotted with red ink the child gets discouraged. Use a different coloured pen to check mistakes. Try to mark only those mistakes that are from the lesson taught recently or currently, and not those spellings learnt in the previous chapter.

Write clearly the correct spellings alongside the spelling mistakes so that corrections can be made. Each spelling should be rewritten by the child at least five times. After this has been done, ask the child to cover the word and write the word from memory. Remember not to compel the whole written exercise to be repeated, as it discourages the child. Piecemeal repetitions are better. For example, out of four paragraphs ask only two to be rewritten. The other two can be part of homework assignment. If some work can be converted into another form, say an essay, it would be more interesting for the child.

Write clearly on the blackboard so that copying is easy. If the child has difficulty in copying from the blackboard, then allow the book to be open for copying. Try using copying task from sources other than the textbook, for example newspaper, scientific magazines, etc.

So, these are some suggestions you can incorporate if you have a child with LD in your class.

Dear teachers, as Carl Jung has rightly said, 'The curriculum is so much necessary raw material, but warmth is the vital element for the growing plant and for the soul of the child.'[1] Teachers, who are alternative caregivers, knowledge-givers and role models, need to emphasize to the learning-disabled child that learning may not be easy, but it still can be worthwhile.

In ancient times the wisdom and strength of the gurukuls did not lie in imparting knowledge alone, but in preparing the child to lead a fruitful, socially relevant and principled life. Your challenges are similar, as—'Teachers who inspire, know that teaching is like cultivating a garden and those who would have nothing to do with thorns must never attempt to gather flowers.' (Unknown Author)

10
Disability as Defined by Law

THE POIGNANT LINES of Wilfred Owen describe the trials and tribulations of persons with any kind of disability:[1]

Some cheered him home, but not as crowds cheer Goal. Only a solemn man who brought him fruits
Thanked him; and then inquired about his soul.

Now, he will spend a few sick years in institutes, And do what things the rules consider wise,
And take whatever pity they may dole.

These solemn words compel us to think that disability of any kind—whether physical or mental or both—leaves a remarkable effect on the psyche of the person. Owen had written the poem describing his physical disability, but it irked his mental prowess when his confidence, autonomy and his very freedom was challenged. This small excerpt from the poem vividly portrays the sense of despondency, despair and desolation.

Disability, as we all know, can be present from birth or may be acquired during one's lifetime. Since disability is not a unilateral phenomenon but encompasses many issues, an attempt has been made by World Health Organization (WHO) to define it in umbrella terms. In 1976, it provided a three-fold definition using the three concepts of impairment, disability and handicap. The WHO proposed:

> an impairment is any loss or abnormality of psychological, physiological or anatomical structure or function; a disability is any restriction or lack (resulting from an impairment) of ability to perform an activity in the manner or within the range considered normal for a human being; a handicap is a disadvantage for a given individual, resulting from an impairment or a disability, that prevents the fulfilment of a role that is considered normal (depending on age, sex, social and cultural factors) for that individual.[2]

Thus, the term disability covered:

> impairments, activity limitations, and participation restrictions. Impairment is a problem in body function or structure; an activity limitation is a difficulty encountered by an individual in executing a task or action; while a participation restriction is a problem experienced by an individual in involvement in life situations and handicap was societal disadvantages due to any disabilities.

International Human Rights

The UN Charter of 1945 proposed creation of certain conditions to bring about stability and well-being amongst nations. This was to promote friendly relations based on the principles of equal rights and self-determination.

Disability, however, officially found its status in 1975, on 9 December, when the General Assembly of the United Nations announced the 'Declaration on the Rights of Disabled Persons'.[3] Taking a leaf out of the UN Charter, it was asserted that the disabled person shall have the same Fundamental Rights as follows:[4]

i. enjoy all rights contained in this declaration without distinction or discrimination

ii. have inherent rights to respect for human dignity and irrespective of the origin, nature and seriousness of the handicap and disabilities

iii. have same civil and political rights

iv. entitlement to measures to make them self-reliant as far as possible

v. right to economic and social security

vi. right to secure and retain employment or engage in useful, productive and remunerative occupation including being a member of the trade unions

vii. right to live with their families or foster parents

viii. right to participate in all social, creative and recreational activities and

ix. right to be protected against exploitation, discrimination, abuse or degradation.

The United Nations went further by declaring 1983–1992 as the Decade of Disabled Persons.[5] Taking cue from a meeting of the Economic and Social Commission for Asia and the Pacific convened at Beijing in 1992, a proclamation on the

Full Participation and Equality of People with Disabilities was made in the declaration of Asian and Pacific Decade of Disabled Persons, 1993–2002. The two decades were instrumental in creating awareness about disabilities and their challenges. Many countries were signatories, including India.

The UN General Assembly additionally passed a resolution in continuation of advocacy for specific disability in December 2001 by establishing an Ad Hoc Committee 'to consider proposals for a comprehensive and integral international convention to promote and protect the rights and dignity of persons with disabilities, based on the holistic approach in the work done in the field of social development, human rights and non-discrimination'.[6]

This brings us to the importance of status of disability laws in India.

Constitutional Rights of Persons with Disability in India

The Constitution of India, which is based on the principles of social justice and human rights, has premised certain provisions given in its Preamble, the Directive Principles of State Policy and the Fundamental Rights. The Preamble uses the words 'Equality' (thereby indicating equality of status and of opportunity) and 'Fraternity' (that assures the dignity of the individual as well as the unity and integrity of the nation).

The Directive Principles of State Policy in Article 41 elaborate that: 'The State shall, within the limits of its economic capacity and development, make effective provision for securing the right to work, to education and to public assistance in cases of unemployment, old age, sickness and disablement.'

The above principles encompassed disability as well. The first ten Five-Year Plans referred to disability, though not directly and prominently. In 1976, a scheme of integrated education for disabled children was introduced, and a year later in 1977, a policy for reservation in jobs for the disabled was introduced. As said earlier, after being a signatory country for Proclamation on the Full Participation and Equality of People with Disabilities in the Asian and Pacific Region, comprehensive laws—like, the Persons with Disabilities (Equal Opportunities, Protection of Rights and Full Participation) Act1995—were made.[7]

The Mental Health Act 1987

The Mental Health Act though was formed before the Human Rights Act had endeavoured to ensure dignity and avoid exploitation of mentally ill persons.[8] The following provisions were already in place, in Section 81 of the Mental Health Act 1987, namely:[9]

1. No mentally ill person shall be subjected during treatment to any indignity (whether physical or mental) or cruelty.
2. No mentally ill person under treatment shall be used for purposes of research, unless—
   i. Such research is of direct benefit to him for purpose of diagnosis or treatment, or
   ii. Such persons, being a voluntary patient has given his consent in writing or where such person (whether or not a voluntary patient) is incompetent by reason minority or otherwise, to give valid consent, the guardian or other person competent to give consent on his behalf, has given his consent in writing for such research.

However, the legislation had emphasized the qualification and appointment of authorities; the admission and discharge of mentally ill persons from specialized institutions; the removal and the role of medical officers, magistrates and police officials; the cost of treatment and liability; and penalties and punishments. All of this gave undue powers to the authorities and there was difficulty in actual implementation of the law.

The Rehabilitation Council of India Act 1992

The Rehabilitation Council of India (RCI) came into existence in 1986. Its role was to regulate and standardize training policies and programmes for the rehabilitation of disabled persons. The need for such a council arose as it was realized and recognized that the persons involved in rehabilitation were not professionally qualified to educate, vocationally train or counsel persons with disabilities. The fallout of this was poor academic and training standards, which took away any chance to compete and procure jobs or vocations, thereby affecting the employability and independent sustenance of the disabled. Thus, an Act of Parliament in 1992 gave more power and enhanced the status of the RCI to a statutory body proclaiming the following aims:

1. To standardize training courses for professionals dealing with people with disabilities;
2. To prescribe minimum standards of education and training of various categories of professionals dealing with people with disabilities;
3. To regulate these standards in all training institutions uniformly throughout the country;
4. To promote research in rehabilitation and special education; and
5. To maintain Central Rehabilitation Register for registration of professionals.

With these powers, now the RCI actively regulates training standards for sixteen categories of rehabilitation workers, and promotes training and research initiatives both for the specialized professional and reputed academic institutions.

Current Legislation for Learning Disability

Learning disability has been recognized in the Rights of Persons with Disability Bill 2014, along with 'autism spectrum disorder, low vision, blindness, cerebral palsy, deaf blindness, haemophilia, hearing impairment, leprosy cured person, intellectual disability, mental illness, loco motor disability, muscular dystrophy, multiple sclerosis, specific learning disabilities, speech and language disability, sickle cell disease, thalassemia, chronic neurological conditions and multiple disability'.[10]

The bill states and recognizes that Specific Learning Disability (SLD) is a heterogeneous group of conditions wherein there is a deficit in processing language, spoken or written, that may be evident as difficulty in comprehension, speech, reading, spelling, writing or mathematical calculations, and includes conditions such as perceptual disabilities, dyslexia, dysgraphia, dyscalculia, etc.

Despite the recognition of the disability, the central government has only given general guidelines for certification to gauge the extent of disability in a person:

1. The appropriate Government will designate persons having requisite qualifications and experience, as certifying authorities who will be competent to issue the certificate of disability.

2. The appropriate Government will also notify the jurisdiction within which and the terms and conditions

subjected to which, the certifying authority shall perform its certification.[11]

However, the bill does not specify any guidelines about the diagnosis, assessment, certification and remediation/rehabilitation pertinent or tailormade for the person with SLD.

Interestingly, in India, only four states, namely Karnataka, Maharashtra, Kerala and Delhi, have recognized disability and been proactive in identification and certification as well as given guidelines and exemptions.

In Karnataka, National Institute of Mental Health and Neurosciences (NIMHANS) took the initiative to develop an index to assess children with LD.[12]

Apart from NIMHANS, St. John's Hospital, Bengaluru and the All-India Institute of Speech and Hearing, Mysuru can certify the child with LD. The final signatures need to be of any psychiatrist working in a government hospital, or any clinical psychologist with an MPhil in medical and social psychology.

In Maharashtra, three hospitals can certify persons as having LD. They are Lokmanya Tilak Municipal Medical College, Mumbai Sion Hospital and Nair Hospital. Two more options have been added by giving authority to KEM Hospital, Mumbai, and the Government Surgeon General in Mumbai.

In Kerala, though the tests are administered by clinical psychologists, but the final signatory is a psychiatrist or a doctor with the rank above assistant surgeon. The request for test administration and final submission of report is in the hands of the school principal. This system is under review due to discrepancies.

In Delhi, the administration gives paediatricians, psychiatrists, clinical psychologists and even special educators the power to certify persons as having LD. However, the assessments are largely done by clinical psychologists and, in some cases, by the special educators. Currently, the certification is done by the Institute of Human Behavioural and Allied Sciences (IBHAS). Delhi has provided relief to the learning disabled even at higher education/ university level under the Persons with Disability scheme. Any person with 40 per cent and above disability will be entitled to reservation in 3 per cent horizontal quota in both reserved and unreserved or general category.

Goa has also decided to acknowledge disability and has tried to promote education by giving financial benefits like transport, uniform allowances, etc. All the five states have tried to work on the principle of inclusion.

Exemptions

Central Board of Secondary Education and Indian Certificate of Secondary Education have both worked on giving some exemptions to school children. The CBSE has allowed the following:[13]

i. use of a scribe. However, the scribe has to be junior, that is, from a lower class;

ii. extra 60 minutes for 3-hour examination, 40 minutes for 2-hour examinations and 30 minutes for 1.5-hour examination;

iii. exemption from the second and third languages without taking another subject in lieu;

iv. questions read aloud but not explained to the student by a reader;

v. use of calculator for children with dyscalculia which the board itself provides to the child;

vi.   exemption from some difficult subjects, taking easier ones in lieu of them; and

vii. can take any four subjects in addition to one compulsory language.

The ICSE also has similar guidelines for dyslexia, dyscalculia, dysgraphia and attention deficit hyperactive disorder candidates:[14]

i.   It gives extra time of 15 minutes for a 1-hour paper, 30 minutes for 2-hour paper and 45 minutes for 3-hour paper;

ii.   Exemption from second language without taking another subject in lieu;

iii. Use of scribe or reader or scribe cum reader who is a grade below the learning-disabled student. The reader can only read the question and is not allowed to explain the question;

iv.   Scribes have to be arranged by the head of the school, in consultation with the convenor and the supervising examiner for the candidate;

v.   Only Casio fx 82 MS calculators are allowed for LD students;

vi.   In some cases, the LD candidate can type the answers;

vii. Provision for answering the examination from hospital is present.

Apart from these concessions, ICSE also follows Affiliation Rules, Chapter III, as mandatory for certain infrastructure:

a)   School buildings to have ramps and lifts;

b) Mandatory to have a counsellor and/or special educator in school;

c) Provision for differently abled students.

However, the acceptance of disability, provisions given by law and its implementation paints a rather dismal picture for a country as large and diverse as India. There is neither a national policy nor workable guidelines to safeguard the interests of persons with LD. A lot needs to be done at the national level, with participation of each state and Union Territory. Only a collective effort can bring about any substantial change in dealing with disability.

A couple of quotes from Albert Einstein, to encourage all the learning-disabled children, their parents and teachers:

'Everybody is a genius. But if you judge a fish by its ability to climb a tree, it will live its whole life believing that it is stupid.'

He further said, *'I'm thankful to those who said NO. Because of them I did it myself.'*

Acknowledgements

A PROVERB OFT-QUOTED BY my schoolteachers was: 'An idle mind is the devil's workshop.' This time I feel that the devil played errant and the nonchalantly thrown seeds, supposedly on an infertile mind during the pandemic lockdown, resulted in a tiny seed struggling to germinate. It was a brave seed that managed to live and thrive well enough to bear fruit in the form of this book.

During the lockdown, umpteen number of parents called up to discuss the difficulties they were facing with their learning-disabled (LD) child. From the inability to follow instructions to writing down notes, sitting for long hours glued to the computers to n number of such difficulties, spoke volumes. Their poignant stories were another source of inspiration for this book. I owe gratitude to the multitude of parents who gave me sufficient experience to gather the courage to write this book.

My gratitude to Dr Rajeev Dhavan, Senior Advocate, Supreme Court of India, who gave me the insight to add a chapter on Disability Laws of India, pertaining to learning disability—as there is a lacuna of information among the general public and very often amongst parents too.

To complete this book, I owe gratitude to many doctors. Without their help and prompt support this book could not have seen the light of day. The medical team of Dr C. Balakrishnan, Dr Vivek Shetty, Dr Shashwat and Dr Ashley for relieving me of pain post Covid. My partner-in-writing and close friend, Dr Mary Abraham, for her support through the thick and thin of life. Dr Lakshmi Vas for her invaluable advice. Dr Jyoti Jain and Dr Savyasachi Saxena who make themselves available to me at a single message. Dr Shreya, my physiotherapist for making me mobile. Many thanks dear doctors.

Some people bend backwards to help and accommodate. I, too, have such wonderful people in my life. Special thanks to my cousins, Shubhra and Anupam Varma, for being pillars of support and accommodating in my hour of need.

No book can be written without one's family's cooperation, emotional support and sharing of labour. I wish to thank my husband Navin, for supporting me by giving constructive and incisive criticism, my elder daughter Shreya, for reading and correcting the drafts of this book and my younger daughter Srishti, for forever helping me to bounce ideas by patiently listening and giving constructive suggestions.

Special thanks to my sister Ranjana and nephew Abhijeet for keeping me sane and happy while working on the book.

Additional References

1. Bakhurst, David. (2005). 'Bruner, Jerome.' *Encyclopedia of Human Development.*

2. Carey, William B. (2004). *Understanding Your Child's Temperament.* Xlibris.

3. Chess, Stella, and Alexander Thomas. (1996). *Temperament*, p. 31. Routledge.

4. Erikson, Erik H., and Erikson, Joan M. (1998). *The Life Cycle Completed: Extended Version.* W. W. Norton.

5. Kohlberg, Lawrence. (1976). 'Moral stages and moralization: The cognitive-developmental approach.' In Thomas Lickona (Ed.), *Moral Development and Behaviour: Theory, Research and Social Issues.* Rinehart and Winston.

6. Kohnstamm, G.A., J.E. Bates, and M.K. Rothbart (Eds). (1989). *Temperament in Childhood*, pp. 59–73. John Wiley and Sons.

7. Rogers, Carl R. (1959). 'A Theory of Therapy, Personality, and Interpersonal Relationships as Developed in the Client-Centered Framework.' In Sigmund Koch (Ed.), *Psychology: A Story of a Science*, vol. 3: pp. 184–256. McGraw-Hill.

8.   Michael, David, and Sande Chen. (2006). *Serious Games: Games That Educate, Train and Transform*. Thomson Course Technology.

1.   Phillips, Denis C., and Jonas F. Soltis. (2009). *Perspectives on Learning. Thinking about Education*. 5th ed. Teachers College Press.

2.   Skinner, B.F. (1953). *Science and Human Behavior*. MacMillan

3.   Willingham, Daniel T., Elizabeth M. Hughes, and David G. Dobolyi. (2015). 'The scientific status of learning styles theories.' *Teaching of Psychology* 42, no. 3: pp. 266–271.

4.   Wolf, Patricia. (2010). *Brain Matters: Translating Research into Classroom Practice* (2nd ed.). ASCD.

5.   Muthukumar, K., M.G. Shashikiran, S. Srinath. (1999). 'A study of co-morbid disorders in children and adolescents presenting with scholastic backwardness.' Paper presented at the 5th IACAM Conference, Bengaluru, 1999.

6.   Das, J.P. (1998). *Dyslexia and Reading Difficulties: An Interpretation for Teachers*. The Maharashtra Dyslexia Association.

7.   Government of Goa. (2005). *Scheme of Education of Children with Special Needs*. Government of Goa.

8.   Government of India. (2003). *Responding to Children with Special Needs: A Manual for Planning and Implementation of Inclusive Education in Sarva Shiksha Abhiyan*. Accessed April 2006; Available from: http://ssa.nic.in/childspl/ssa_plan_ manual.pdf

9.   National Centre for Learning Disabilities. (2006). 'Response to Intervention.' Accessed September 2006. Available from: http://www.ncld.org/content/view/1002/389/

10. National Institute of Open Schooling. (2006) 'Indian Open Schooling Network (IOSN): Web Linking of Schools.' Accessed March 2006. Available from: http://www.nios.ac.in/iosn.htm

11. National Joint Commission on Learning Disabilities. (2005). *Responsiveness to Intervention and Learning Disability*. Accessed

September 2006. Available from: http://www.ldanatl.org/pdf/ rti2005. pdf#search=%22Response%20to%

12. Individuals with Disabilities Education Act. (2004). Accessed April 2006. Available from: URL:http://frwebgate.access. gpo. gov.cgibin/getdoc.cgi?dbname=108_cong_public_ laws&docid=f:publ446.108

13. Reid, L., Tom H., Andrew H., and Ann K. (1994). 'Washington Summit on Learning Disabilities. Notes on the Summary Report.' Accessed March 2006. Available from: http:// www.ldhope.com/ wash.html

14. Sadock, Benjamin J., Harold I. Kaplan, and Virginia A. Sadock. (2007). *Kaplan & Sadock's Synopsis of Psychiatry: Behavioral SciencesClinical Psychiatry.* 10th ed. Wolter Kluwer/Lippincott Williams & Wilkins.

15. Eagleson, Catherine, Simon Hayed, Andrew Mathews, G. Perman, and Christopher R. Hirsch. (2016). 'The Power of Positive Thinking: Pathological Worry Is Reduced by Thought Replacement in Generalized Anxiety Disorder.' *Behaviour Research and Therapy* 78: pp. 13–18. https://doi. org/10.1016/j. brat.2015.12.017

Notes

Sweety

1. For greater understanding of phonetics and phonemes please refer to Section III, Chapter 7 in this book.
2. In brief, phonetics deal with two aspects of speech-production (the sounds made) and perception (the way speech is understood). 'Phoneme' refers to the smallest unit of sound that can differentiate the meaning as sounds uttered when a letter (e.g., cap, kite, job, etc.), or combination of letters (e.g., chime, kitchen, ring, sleep, mouse, cow, etc.) are pronounced.

1: Developmental Growth

1. Thomas, Alexander, Stella Chess, and Herbert G. Birch. (1970). 'The Origin of Personality.' *Scientific American* 223, no. 2: pp. 102–09.

2. Chess, Stella, and Alexander Thomas. (1990). 'Continuities and Discontinuities in Temperament.' In Lee N. Robins and Michael Rutter (Eds), *Straight and Devious Pathways from Childhood to Adulthood*, pp. 205–220. Cambridge University Press.

3. Piaget, Jean. (1977). 'The Role of Action in the Development of Thinking.' In Willis F. Overton and John M. Gallagher (Eds), *Knowledge and Development*, pp. 17–42. Springer.

4. Rogers, Carl. (1959). 'A Theory of Therapy, Personality and Interpersonal Relationships as Developed in the Client-centered Framework.' In Sigmund Koch (Ed.), *Psychology: A Study of a Science*, vol. 3: *Formulations of the Person and the Social Context*. McGraw Hill.

5. Erikson, Erik. (1956). 'The Problem of Ego Identity.' *Journal of the American Psychoanalytic Association* 4, pp. 56–121. https://www.sci-hub.se/10.1177/000306515600400104

6. Kohlberg, Lawrence. (1976). 'Moral Stages and Moralization: The Cognitive-Developmental Approach.' In Thomas Lickona (Ed.), *Moral Development and Behavior: Theory, Research and Social Issues*. Rinehart and Winston.

2: Learning Concepts

1. Hilgard, Ernest R., Richard C. Atkinson and Rita L. Atkinson. (1979). *Introduction to Psychology*, 7th ed. Harcourt.

2. Thorndike, Edward L. (1914). *Education Psychology*. Routledge.

3. Thorndike, Edward L. (1932). *The Fundamentals of Learning*. Teachers College Press.

4. Gardner, Howard. (2006). *Multiple Intelligences: New Horizons in Theory and Practice*. Basic Books.

5. Chomsky, Noam. (1965). *Aspects of the Theory of Syntax*. MIT Press.

6.   Pavlov, Ivan P. (1927). 'Conditioned Reflexes: An Investigation of the Physiological Activity of the Cerebral Cortex.' Translated by G.V. Anrep. *Nature* 121 (3052), pp. 662–664.

7.   Skinner, B.F. (1953). *Science and Human Behavior*. MacMillan.

3: Learning Disability

1.   National Joint Committee on Learning Disabilities. (1998). 'Operationalizing the NJCLD Definition of Learning Disabilities for Ongoing Assessment in Schools.' *Asha* 40 (Suppl. 18).

2.   Misquitta, Raveena, and A. Panshikar. (2022). 'Identification of Learning Disabilities in India: Current Challenges and Issues.' *Intervention in School and Clinic* 58, no. 3 (2003): pp. 213–217. https://doi. org/10.1177/10534512221081274

3.   Shah, H.R., J.K.V. Sagar, M.P. Somaiya, and J.K. Nagpal. (2019). 'Clinical Practice Guidelines on Assessment and Management of Specific Learning Disorders.' *Indian Journal of Psychiatry* 61, pp. 211–225. https://doi.org/10.4103/psychiatry.

4.   Kuriyan, N.M., J. Reddy, and J.K. James. (2019). 'Prevalence of Learning Disability and Emotional Problems Among Children: An Overview of Emotion and Creativity Focused Interventions.' *The International Journal of Psychosocial Rehabilitation* 22, no. 2: pp. 22–31.

5.   Rehabilitation Council of India. (n.d.). 'Learning Disabilities.' http://www.rehabcouncil.nic.in/writereaddata/ld.pdf

6.   Reid, L., Tom H., Andrew H., and Ann K. (1994). 'Washington Summit on Learning Disabilities: Notes on the Summary Report.' http://www.ldhope.com/wash.html

4: Types of Academic Skills Disorders

1. Sadock, Benjamin J., Virginia A. Sadock, and Pedro Ruiz. (2017). *Kaplan & Sadock's Comprehensive Textbook of Psychiatry.* 10th ed. Wolter Kluwer/Lippincott Williams & Wilkins.

2. Sadock, Benjamin J., Virginia A. Sadock, and Pedro Ruiz (Eds). (2017). *Kaplan & Sadock's Comprehensive Textbook of Psychiatry.* 10th ed. Wolter Kluwer/Lippincott Williams & Wilkins.

3. Ibid.

4. Kosc, Ladislav. (1970). 'Psychology and Psychopathology of Mathematical Abilities.' *Studia Psychologica* 12, pp. 159–162.

5. Rubinstein, Orly and Avishai Henik. (2009). 'Developmental Dyscalculia: Heterogeneity May Not Mean Different Mechanisms.' *Trends in Cognitive Sciences*, 13, pp. 92–99.

6. Piazza, Manuela. (2010). 'Neurocognitive Start-up Tools for Symbolic Number Representations.' *Trends in Cognitive Science* 14, pp. 542–551. https://doi. org/10.1016/j.tics.2010.09.008

7. Keeler, Mary L., and H. Lee Swanson. (2001). 'Does Strategy Knowledge Influence Working Memory in Children with Mathematical Disabilities?' *Journal of Learning Disabilities* 34, no. 5: pp. 418–434; Swanson, H. Lee. (2004). 'Working Memory and Phonological Processing as Predictors of Children's Mathematical Problem Solving at Different Ages.' *Memory & Cognition* 32, no. 4: pp. 648–661; and, Bull, Rebecca, Kimberly A. Espy, and Sabrina A. Weibe. (2008). 'Short-term Memory, Working Memory, and Executive Functioning in Preschoolers: Longitudinal Predictors of Mathematical Achievement at Age 7 Years.' *Developmental Neuropsychology* 33, no. 3: pp. 205–228.

8. Rourke, Byron P. (1993). 'Arithmetic Disabilities, Specific and Otherwise.' *Journal of Learning Disabilities* 26, pp. 214–226; Rourke, Byron P., and John A. Conway. (1997). 'Disabilities of Arithmetic and Mathematical Reasoning: Perspectives from

Neurology and Neuropsychology.' *Journal of Learning Disabilities* 30, no. 1: pp. 34–46.

9. Blair, Clancy. (2006). 'How Similar Are Fluid Cognition and General Intelligence? A Developmental Neuroscience Perspective on Fluid Cognition as an Aspect of Human Cognitive Ability.' *Behavioral and Brain Sciences* 29, pp. 109–60; Bull, Rebecca, and Gema Scerif. (2001). 'Executive Functioning as a Predictor of Children's Mathematics Ability: Inhibition, Switching, and Working Memory.' *Developmental Neuropsychology* 19, pp. 273–293; Bull, Rebecca, Robert S. Johnston, and Jean A. Jean. (1999). 'Exploring the Roles of the Visual-Spatial Sketchpad and Central Executive in Children's Arithmetical Skills: Views from Cognition and Developmental Neuropsychology.' *Developmental Neuropsychology* 15: pp. 421–442; Espy, Kimberly A., Marcia M. McDiarmid, Melissa F. Cwik, Matthew M. Stalets, Aimee Hamby, and T. E. Senn. (2004). 'The Contribution of Executive Functions to Emergent Mathematical Skills in Preschool Children.' *Developmental Neuropsychology* 26: pp. 465–486; McKenzie, Brent, Rebecca Bull, and Clare Gray. (2003). 'The Effects of Phonological and Visual-Spatial Interference on Children's Arithmetical Performance.' *Educational and Child Psychology* 20, no. 3: pp. 93–108; Passolunghi, Maria Chiara, Cesare Cornoldi, and Stefano De Liberto. (1999). 'Working Memory and Inhibition of Irrelevant Information in Poor Problem Solvers.' *Memory & Cognition* 27, pp. 779–790; and, Passolunghi, Maria Chiara, and Linda S. Siegel. (2004). 'Working Memory and Access to Numerical Information in Children with Disabilities in Mathematics.' *Journal of Experimental Child Psychology* 88, no. 4: pp. 348–367.

10. Phonics and phonemes are discussed in detail in Section III, Chapter 7. 'Management of Learning Disability.'

11. Reynolds, Cecil, and Elaine Fletcher-Janzen. (2007). *Encyclopedia of Special Education: A Reference for the Education of Children, Adolescents, and Adults with Disabilities and other Exceptional Individuals.* 3rd ed. John Wiley & Sons.

12. Overvelde, Annemiek, and Wouter Hulstijn. (2011). 'Handwriting Development in Grade 2 and Grade 3 Primary School Children with Normal, At Risk, or Dysgraphic Characteristics.' *Research in Developmental Disabilities* 32, no. 2: pp. 540–548.

13. Sadock, Benjamin J., Virginia A. Sadock, and Pedro Ruiz. (2017). *Kaplan & Sadock's Comprehensive Textbook of Psychiatry.* 10th ed. Wolter Kluwer/Lippincott Williams & Wilkins.

14. Mogasale, Vittal V., Venkatesh D. Patil, N. M. Patil, et al. (2012). 'Prevalence of Specific Learning Disabilities among Primary School Children in a South Indian City.' *Indian J Pediatr* 79, pp. 342–347. https://doi.org/10.1007/s12098-011-0553-3.

15. Baldwin, James Mark. (1896). 'A New Factor in Evolution.' *The American Naturalist* 30 (354): pp. 441–451.

6: Assessment of Learning Disability

1. Bender, William N. (2008). *Learning Disabilities: Characteristics, Identification, and Teaching Strategies.* Allyn & Bacon.

2. Wechsler, David. (2014). *Wechsler Intelligence Scale for Children.* 5th ed. Pearson.

3. Malin, A.J. (1969). 'Malin's Intelligence Scale for Children Manual.' Indian Psychological Corporation.

4. Roid, Gale H. (2003). *Stanford-Binet Intelligence Scales.* 5th Ed. Riverside Publishing.

5. Ibid.

6. Kamat, V.V. (1967). *Measuring Intelligence of Indian Children.* 4th ed. Oxford University Press.

7.   Wilkinson, Gary S., and Gary J. Robertson. (2017). *Wide Range Achievement Test 5*. Psychological Assessment Resources. Pearson

8.   Ibid.

9.   Hirisave, Uma, Asha Oommen, and M. Kapur. (2006). *Psychological Assessment of Children in the Clinical Setting. NIMHANS Index of Specific Learning Disabilities*. Samudra Offset Printers.

10. Ibid.

11. Woodcock, Richard W., Kevin S. McGrew, and Nancy Mather. (2001). *Examiner's Manual. Woodcock-Johnson. Tests of Cognitive Ability*. 3rd ed. Riverside Publishing.

12. Kaufman, Alan S., and Nadeen L. Kaufman. (2004). *Kaufman Assessment Battery for Children*. 2nd ed. American Guidance Service.

13. Battle, James. (2002). *Culture-free Self-Esteem Inventory*. 3rd ed. Ann Arbour Publishers.

14. Kovacs, Maria. (2010). *Children's Depression Inventory*. 2nd ed. Pearson. Accessed February 18, 2014. https://www.pearsonassessments.com/en-us/Store/Professional-Assessments/Personality-6-Biopsychosocial/Children7s-Depression-Inventory-2/p/100000636

15. Kovacs, Maria, and MHS Staff. (2011). *Children's Depression Inventory Second Edition (CDI 2): Technical Manual*. Multi-Health Systems.

16. Spielberger, Charles D., Cynthia D. Edwards, Joseph Montouri, and Robert Lushene. (1973). *State-Trait Anxiety Inventory for Children (STAI-CH)*. APA PsycTests. https://doi.org/10.1037/t06497-000

17. Birmaher, Boris, David A. Brent, Lauren Chiappetta, Jeffrey Bridge, Suneeta Monga, and Michael Baugher. (1999). 'Psychometric Properties of the Screen for Child Anxiety Related Emotional Disorders (SCARED): A Replication Study.' *Journal of*

the American Academy of Child & Adolescent Psychiatry 38, no. 10: pp. 1230–1236.

18. Spielberger, Charles D., Cynthia D. Edwards, Joseph Montouri, and Robert Lushene. (1973). *State-Trait Anxiety Inventory for Children (STAI-CH)*. APA PsycTests. https://doi.org/10.1037/t06497-000

19. Bellak, Leopold, and Sonya S. Bellak (1949). 1991. *Children's Apperception Test: Manual*. 8th rev. ed. C.P.S.

20. Bellak, Leopold, and Sonya S. Bellak. (1994). *Children's Apperception Test—Human Figures* (CAT-H). 11th ed. C.P.S.

21. Bellak, Leopold. (1992). *The T.A.T., C.A.T., and S.A.T. in Clinical Use*. 5th ed. Allyn & Bacon.

22. Goodenough, Florence. (1926). *Measurement of Intelligence by Drawings*. World Book Co.

23. Machover, Karen. (1949). *Personality Projection in the Drawing of a Human Figure*. Charles C. Thomas Publisher.

24. Rotter, Julian B., Janet E. Rafferty. (1950). The Rotter Incomplete Sentences Blank. Manual, College Form. The Psychological Corporation.Notes

25. Rorschach, Hermann. (1927). *Rorschach Test—Psychodiagnostic Plates*. Hogrefe Publishing Corp.

7: Management of Learning Disability

1. Das, J.P. (2005). *PASS Reading Enhancement Program: Revised Research Edition*. University of Alberta.

2. Das, J.P., Jack A. Naglieri, and John R. Kirby. (1994). *Assessment of Cognitive Processes*. Allyn & Bacon.

3. Mercer, Cecil D., Margo K. Rudolph, and Richard G. Wilson. (1998). *Merrill Reading Program—Step Up Teacher Edition—Level E*. Mcgraw-Hill Books.

4. Dewsbury, Anne. (1983). *Bridge Reading Kit*. OISE Press.

5. Fernald, Grace M. (1988). L. Idol (Ed.) *Remedial Techniques in Basic School Subjects*. Pro-Ed.

6. Robinson, Francis Pleasant. (1978). *Effective Study*. 6th ed. Harper & Row.

7. Learning Strategies Center, Cornell University. *The Cornell Note-Taking System*. Cornell University.

8. Axline, Virginia. (1969). *Play Therapy*. Rev. ed. Ballantine Books.

9. Jacobson, Edmund. (1938). *Progressive Relaxation*. University of Chicago Press.

10. Wolpe, Joseph. (1958). *Psychotherapy by Reciprocal Inhibition*. Stanford University Press.

11. Beck, Aaron T. (1967). *The Diagnosis and Management of Depression*. University of Pennsylvania Press.

8: A Note for Parents

1. Waitley, Denis (1933–2025) was a retired US naval aviator, an author, motivational speaker and consultant. The quote above is not dated, but is thought to be taken from one of his speeches. https://en.wikipedia.org/wiki/Denis_Waitley#:~:text=Denis%20 E.,International%20Speakers'%20Hall%20of%20Fame.

9: A Note for Teachers

1. Jung, Carl. (1963). *Memories, Dreams, Reflections*, p. 101. Random House.

10: Disability as Defined by Law

1. Owen, Wilfred. (1920). *Poems*. Chatto & Windus. https://www. sas.upenn.edu/~cavitch/pdf-library/Owen_Poems_1920_edition. pdf

2.   World Health Organization. (1976). *International Classification of Impairments, Disabilities, and Handicaps: A Manual of Classification Relating to the Consequences of Disease.* World Health Organization.

3.   United Nations. 1975. *Declaration on the Rights of Disabled Persons.* Adopted by General Assembly Resolution 3447 (XXX), December 9, 1975.

4.   Ibid.

5.   UN General Assembly. 1984. United Nations Decade of Disabled Persons: Resolution Adopted by the General Assembly, November 23, 1984. A/RES/39/26. https://www.refworld.org/docid/3b00f4 762e.html

6.   United Nations, Ad Hoc Committee on a Comprehensive and Integral International Convention on Protection and Promotion of the Rights and Dignity of Persons with Disabilities. 2003. *Report of the Ad Hoc Committee,* June 16–27, 2003. https://www. un.org/esa/socdev/enable/rights/a_58_118_e.htm

7.   Government of India. 1995. Persons with Disabilities (Equal Opportunities, Protection of Rights and Full Participation) Act. Accessed January 27, 2017. http://www.disabilityaffairs.gov.in upload/uploadfiles/files/PWD_Act.pdf

8.   The Mental Health Act, 1987. (1987). *The Gazette of India.* https:// www.wbhealth.gov.in/mental_health/Acts_Rules/MHA_1987. pdf

9.   Ibid.

10. PRS Legislative Research. 2014. The Right of Persons with Disabilities Bill, 2014, as introduced in the Rajya Sabha. Accessed 10 October 2014. http://www.prsindia.org/billtrack/the-right-of-persons-with-disabilities-bill-2014-3122/

11. Government of India. 2018. The Children with Specific Learning Disabilities (Identification and Support in Education) Bill, 2018. A bill to identify and support the children with learning

disabilities in education and for matters connected therewith or incidental thereto.

12. Kapur, M., I.P. Barnabas, M.V. Reddy, J. Rozario, and H. Uma (2002). 'Developmental Psychopathology Checklist for Children (DPCL).' In U. Hirisave, A. Oommen, and M. Kapur (Eds), *Psychological Assessment of Children in the Clinical Setting*, no. 48: pp. 6–53. NIMHANS.

13. Central Board of Secondary Education. https://www.cbse.nic.in.

14. Council for the Indian School Certificate Examinations. https://www.cisce.org.

About the Author

Dr Vandana V. Prakash is a clinical psychologist, neuropsychologist, academician, researcher and trainer, practising for the last thirty-three years. She has an MPhil in medical and social psychology from NIMHANS, Bangalore. Dr Prakash received her doctorate in 'Stress, Perceived Control and Coping Behaviour of Parents of Adjusted and Maladjusted Adolescents'. She has co-authored the books *Conquering Pain: How to Prevent It, Treat It and Lead a Better Life* and *Managing Chronic Pain*. Apart from pain behaviour, she has a special interest in suicidal behaviour and has co-authored chapters on suicidal behaviour amongst adolescents and adults for several international publications.

HarperCollins *Publishers* India

At HarperCollins India, we believe in telling the best stories and finding the widest readership for our books in every format possible. We started publishing in 1992; a great deal has changed since then, but what has remained constant is the passion with which our authors write their books, the love with which readers receive them, and the sheer joy and excitement that we as publishers feel in being a part of the publishing process.

Over the years, we've had the pleasure of publishing some of the finest writing from the subcontinent and around the world, including several award-winning titles and some of the biggest bestsellers in India's publishing history. But nothing has meant more to us than the fact that millions of people have read the books we published, and that somewhere, a book of ours might have made a difference.

As we look to the future, we go back to that one word—a word which has been a driving force for us all these years.

Read.

Harper Collins

Harper Sport

HARPER FICTION

HARPER NON-FICTION

हार्पर हिन्दी

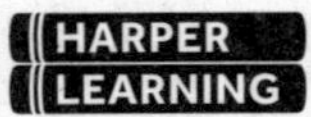

HARPER LEARNING

HARPER VANTAGE

HCCB HARPERCOLLINS CHILDREN'S BOOKS

4th

HARPER PERENNIAL

HARPER DESIGN

BOOKTOPUS

HARPER BUSINESS